Terence Roberts was born in Ruthin, North Wales, but grew up in the old industrial heartlands of West Yorkshire. After joining West Yorkshire Probation Service as a volunteer in the mid 1980s, he later qualified as a probation officer at the University of Huddersfield and then worked for over 25 years in Merseyside, West Yorkshire and the Republic of Ireland.

He moved to Ireland at the age of 50, to work in Limerick city. He is now recently retired and continues to live outside the village of O'Brien's Bridge, County Clare, with his family of retired greyhounds, horses and donkeys.

This is dedicated to all those who have made this journey possible, including my Welsh family and my good friends in Yorkshire and in Ireland. Some of you are hidden in the pages that follow while others are warmly hidden in my thoughts. All of you are very much appreciated, especially John and Mary Crotty. I cannot thank the Crottys enough for everything they have done for me, giving me the opportunity to live this great life in Ireland. They are my Irish family and have always treated me as such.

This work is also dedicated to the carers, those people who care for others and the world we live in, particularly at this difficult time. This includes those who care for the animals that enrich our lives in many ways and who constantly remind us that we are not the only ones worthy of this planet. For those who look after the welfare of greyhounds, this piece of work is a firm acknowledgement of their particular efforts.

Terence Roberts

# ALL BECAUSE OF DAISY

AUSTIN MACAULEY PUBLISHERS™

LONDON • CAMBRIDGE • NEW YORK • SHARJAH

A CIP catalogue record for this title is available from the British Library.

ISBN 9781398413030 (Paperback)
ISBN 9781398413047 (ePub e-book)

www.austinmacauley.com

First Published 2023
Austin Macauley Publishers Ltd®
1 Canada Square
Canary Wharf
London
E14 5AA

Many thanks to those who helped me in a technical capacity to complete this work, namely Paul and Cheryl Roberts, Denis Bartley and John Conway. Your practical advice has been invaluable.

Also, many thanks to my good friend, Yorkshire Paul, for encouraging me to share this story.

# Table of Contents

# Introduction

I moved to Ireland on November 24$^{th}$, 2008, a middle-aged man in search of something. Since then I have often been asked, "What brings you to Ireland?" My usual answer would be, "Well, it's all because of Daisy." Of course life is never so simple. However, my time in Ireland has given me the opportunity to fully consider my route to Ireland and more importantly, why I stay.

Inspiration comes in many guises. Last summer I watched my very good friend, John Crotty, build a kennel for my two greyhounds overlooking the field. I saw a man different from myself and yet similar to myself. I saw a man create something within a few short days that could last for years. I asked myself what I had built. Nothing. I decided there and then that it was time to create and complete something myself, hence this piece of work. My experiences in Ireland have widened and changed my perspectives of life. In telling the tale I hope those, who know me well, will understand why I needed to leave one world for another in search of a dream and why I stayed because of the truth.

# 1 – Love at First Sight

In June 2004 I caught the ferry from Holyhead to Dublin. It was my first visit to Ireland. Those three days on the Emerald Isle changed my life forever.

I was forty-six at the time, employed as a probation officer in West Yorkshire. Mum was alive and kicking at the ripe old age of 81. Dad had passed away five years earlier and brother Ronnie two years after that. I was still just about with Fran, who many people said was the love of my life. Her mother and sister had died close together in the last two years and on reflection, we had experienced enough doom and gloom in a short time. Yet life went on as ever.

Mum's passion were greyhounds ever since Mischievous Girl arrived as a birthday present in 1998. Connie, as she was well-known at her local track, Sheffield, was followed by another ten dogs over the years. Some had been bought as two-year-olds and others as pups. My mother wanted me to check out the latest edition to the family, a five-month-old bitch bred and reared in County Tipperary by Larry Bourke. So, for the first time, I crossed the Irish Sea from Holyhead to Dublin.

I made my way from the boat terminal to Heuston Station under strict instructions to get the train to Limerick Junction, not Limerick city. The instructions came from Larry. Our mutual friend, Brian Gillard, who owned the litter mother, had told Larry that "I didn't have much cop on", which I later found out meant that I was short on common sense. However, I somehow managed to be smart enough to buy the right ticket and get the right train and sat back and watched Ireland by rail unfold. Field to field, filling my eye with trees, lush pasture and horses, the train sped southwest. I noticed that the train was in excellent condition, spacious, new and bright. I also noticed the accents, probably coming from most parts of Ireland. Some I could understand, others just about. What I definitely understood was the sense of warmth of people not afraid to talk to each other. Of grannies proudly talking about their grandchildren, their adventures to work in Canada or their new life in Dublin 'doing something to do with computers'. Then, from Canada to Dublin, the grannies returned to talk about those left behind to do the essential jobs, the milkman, the priest and the teacher who made local scandal with a Polish immigrant. He had rented a flat in a village miles away so that he could provide residential private tuition at no cost to his pretty teenage student…and he hadn't discussed the arrangement with his wife.

I also picked up a tangible passion but I couldn't quite understand the full meaning behind it. Would Kilkenny win the Senior Hurling and what were Kerry's chances in the football? I'd not heard such banter and jesting for many years, in some ways similar to the Wars of the Roses arguments in cricket but the difference being that everyone seemed to be joining in…including the sparky grannies with one proudly saying that her son won an 'All Ireland' in the days before a protective helmet was even invented. There was a passionate flow of words, occasionally broken with gasps and the lifting and rattling of shaking heads. Everyone expressed a pride in their county or the villages where these amateur heroes first made their names. I looked on as an outsider looking in but never felt excluded from the warmth of the fire.

We arrived in Limerick Junction. I recall a handful of people getting off and I followed them down the platform, fields and racing rails to my right. I lumbered down to the exit and spotted a middle-aged man thirty yards away, the only person waiting to pick up a visitor. "Larry?" I asked offering my hand.

"Yes, and you'd be Terry from Yorkshire? Jesus, I was looking for a wee jockey type of a man…that Gillard is a bad one, never believe a tale he tells you." Larry had expected a sprightly eight-stone man to hop off the train instead of a nineteen stone six-footer, built like an out of shape retired rugby player.

It was a good start as I soon felt that this was a man with an easy sense of humour. He asked me the usual sort of questions as we drove to his house, what I did for a living and what car did I drive. He started to ask if I was married but soon added that I couldn't be because I looked too happy to be in that predicament. I had planned to stay in Tipperary town in a Bed and Breakfast but Larry soon threw this out of the window by warmly asking me to stay at his and Babs' home. I readily accepted. Within twenty minutes of driving through a number of small villages and bypassing occasional isolated houses, we arrived at Cappawhite. Opening the car door led to a greeting of barking greyhounds, a sound that I had grown to love in recent years. Acting as security dog was Tyson, a blubbery and affectionate red-boxer, who clearly knew his job was to raise the alarm and give welcoming kisses at the same time. In three paddocks were a host of yappy, noisy greyhounds rushing to the fences and jumping over each other to impress visitors and get affection. For me it was like walking into heaven. Larry ushered me in to the kitchen and introduced me to his wife. I sat down there and then and this 'wee jockey of a man' was introduced to a large plate of chops, potatoes and vegetables, followed by a glass of milk. Babs had heard, no doubt from Brian Gillard, that I was a wee jockey in need of a good meal and my rapid, relentless consumption of that lovely meal surely confirmed it.

Their hospitality was an eye-opener and I graciously thanked them for the meal and the invitation to stay the night. Babs declined the offer of me doing the washing up, hastily pushing me outside with Larry to see the dogs. We went through the first group of greyhounds, all as keen as mustard to get some attention. They looked the happiest dogs. In the next paddock there were two dogs and one bitch from the same litter. The bitch held her own with her muscle – bound brothers, not being afraid to force them from the fence. She walked three yards to the left, then three to the right, repeating the dance every few seconds or so while rubbing her side against the fence all the time. Her tail wagged and wagged like I had never seen before. Her head lifted as though to say look at me, look at me. This was the pup that I had travelled to see. She looked so different from the videos that had been sent by Larry. Her woolly coat was brown and full in texture. She was the brown sheep of the family. Mum had already chosen her racing name, Calon Lan, a classical Welsh hymn exalting a pure heart. I asked Larry what her kennel name was. "Oh, that's Daisy, that's Daisy, all right…yes, she's yours."

I spent another twenty minutes or so watching the dogs, paying particular attention to how Daisy was having great fun with her brothers whilst occasionally rushing down to the fence to say hello again or maybe goodbye. I asked Larry question after question, trying to ascertain how rearing and training were different in Ireland compared to British ways. Soon time was pressing and Larry told me to get my coat as we were going into Limerick to see a dog of his run. Perfect. The drive to Limerick was again through ever-green and beautiful countryside, reminding me of Wales, reminding me of my first home, my family home. There was a real sense of space, of clean and healthy greenness. The talk was of dogs now, not least Larry's love for breeding and rearing and his recollections of selling quality dogs, often to Englishmen. This was a man passionate about his dogs and his way of life. A content man but not a settled man. He was someone who was always thinking of the next litter, the next racing gem that might be discovered.

Soon we arrived on the edge of Limerick city and approached the Market Fields Stadium on Mulgrave Street. Bang opposite were walls that looked familiar, walls that contained and protected. This was Limerick Prison. For a moment work flashed very briefly to mind. Perhaps I had been institutionalised and even conditioned myself, automatically picking up the sense and scent of incarceration, the nuts and bolts of my trade. Yet, thankfully, this was a fleeting glimpse as we turned right into the trainer's car park. Inside were half-a-dozen folk or more, their athletic hounds tied by the lead. They talked and shared views on the nights racing, their dogs having come from kennels all over the county and beyond. We walked to the rear of the car park, looping around the edge of the track which looked perfectly sanded. The track was open and honest, by which I mean it looked like a safe and welcoming track for dogs to hit forty miles at the first bend and to sustain their pace as best they can to the line. We arched around from the second bend to the finishing line where the kennels were. I had never seen such homely and welcoming kennels. They were open to public gaze where greyhounds could be seen being prepared to race and where they were later washed down and proudly cared for after doing their duty. It gave spectators the chance to watch these enthusiastic trainers and owners show what greyhound racing was about, something which doesn't happen in most countries. The atmosphere made me think of a different era, fifty years earlier in England maybe when the sport would have been far, far more important than hospitality and meal deals. It all seemed so relaxed but yet it all seemed so important, if that makes sense. This was real sport, real greyhound racing for people who knew their dogs and their racing.

Larry introduced me to some other trainers and again their talk was purely about the dogs, their preparation, fitness, trap draw and their chances for the night. Their injuries, their litter brothers, their sale price. It reminded me of whippet racing in Yorkshire, real dog people with a real passion for their way of life. One person I met was Mary Crotty, a lovely warm lady who came from a village called O'Brien's Bridge. Mary, Larry and others mingled and chatted and then peeled apart as they each carefully prepared their dogs in their own individual way and then proudly paraded them in front of the crowd. They walked across the field, displaying their hounds like gladiators before the moment of truth. Then the race, the explosion from the traps, the prayers to get around the first bend in a safe and advantageous position. Then the glorious images at each and every bend and on each extended straight when greyhounds showed pace and power and above all else, their heart to win the prize. It was sport at its best and while Larry's dog didn't win, he pleased his owner with a promising run for one so young. After a few more races we said goodbye to Mary and others and sped off back to Larry's, arriving shortly before 10.30 in the evening. It had been a wonderful night.

On arriving back at the house Babs made a cheese sandwich for supper and I was ready and content to pack myself off to bed, my mind already stretched and satisfied after that night at the dogs. Larry had other ideas. Off we went, the three of us into the dark, into the car and into the wilderness. We drove for fifteen minutes, the only lights being from the car and the occasional house. We arrived in a small village of perhaps twenty houses and not a soul in sight. We walked into what I thought was a house, into what I thought was somebody's front room. Maybe ten or twelve people were there, half feeling the warmth of the crackling coal fire, the rest sat together leaning on the bar. Larry and Babs knew them all. I remember having a good night going on until well past 2.00 in the morning. I also remember the humour and warmth, the relaxed atmosphere and I vividly recall that the more people drank, the quicker they spoke and the less I understood! A local politician was sat at the bar, happy to mix community business with refreshing pleasure eventually leading to a rendition of 'The fields of Athenrye'. Tales were told by many of the locals in the room and the trick was to work out which were true and which were told for jest and devilment. I nearly fell in love with the landlady there and then, her jet black hair and dark green eyes being as mesmerising as her saucy smile and teasing wit. I knew that this night was something different. I was not a virgin by any means as far as drinking in pubs was concerned. However, this night was a memorable one. It was my first taste and drink of Ireland. There was a relaxed hospitality and ease about the place where I felt a real sense of comfort amongst people from another world. This commitment to enjoy life to the full, to mix socially without airs and graces getting in the way. This, I was soon to discover, is the Irish way.

I slept well that night. It had been the most unforgettable day for me and it remains so. I felt at home. The next morning I had the best breakfast ever. I had never had white pudding before and the bacon or rashers as they are called, contributed to a wholesome start. I spent the rest of the morning talking dogs with Larry and spending time with Daisy and the other pups. I remember so very, very clearly how happy I was, simply enjoying the company and the rural calm. Larry asked if I would stay a few days more. I couldn't. I needed to get to Dublin where I had booked into a hotel...but I would be back.

So, I made my way to Dublin, again enjoying the journey. I nursed my hangover and occasionally broke out in inner and silent, external smiles as I recalled the night before. Again the expanse of green space from horizon to horizon caught my eye, interspersed occasionally by towns whose names were hard to read and harder to pronounce...Portlaoise, for example. Then the voiceover in the train frequently spurting out what sounded like 'from here-nor-there' but simply proving that this was an independent country with its own identity and language. The beauty was in this independence, this unique character and culture, which hit home within those few, short and enjoyable days.

Dublin was different altogether, as much because one massive city is very much like another. Hustle, bustle, people coming and going and very few staying. It is Irish but cosmopolitan. It has a past which it seems sure of but a future of uncertainty. It's a city which symbolises the greatest victory of freedom but one which struggles to offset yet another generation of social problems. Many say that it's just like any other Irish village with the same social and economic problems but with totally different characters. In the years that followed I managed to see some of Dublin life when I occasionally stayed over including witnessing the throaty rants of 'come on the Dubs' as their football idols tried to regain lost heritage in the Gaelic Games. Dublin people, like Irish people anywhere in the world, are rightly very proud of where they come from. However, on this occasion, my first night in Dublin, I did the tourist thing. I enjoyed a pleasurable evening, much of it alone. Then, back in the loneliness of my hotel room, my mind held on to the past few days as though I had been handed a gift, a precious gift that had already started to widen my horizons. I went to sleep, happily wondering when I'd be back and in what circumstances.

# 2 – A Bridge over the Shannon

I returned home to West Yorkshire the next day with work lurking the day after. I'd recently moved to Liversedge. I'd been with Fran, on and off, for over ten years. Looking back, maybe she was the love of my life after all but I never knew it at the time. I guess that you never know until it is too late. Fran had everything. She always had the looks from the prettiest young woman to the sexiest and classiest mature woman. She had a heart the size of your imagination. She could meet people and engage with them within minutes. She did this effortlessly. This skill and a genuine feeling for people from all worlds made her a wonderful woman. While my mother taught me my better values as a child, Fran taught many of my better values as an adult. She opened my mind up in many ways, somehow enabling me to question things from different perspectives.

After being born in South West England she spent much of her early childhood in India. Her dad, Basil, was a very successful businessman, a good husband and father. He had died some years before Fran and I met and I regret that I never had time to spend with him. I would have learnt a lot. Mum was Mollie, a lovely lady, clear thinking and exuding an innocence and warmth, not an edge to her. Unfortunately,

Mollie developed Alzheimer's and we felt that the move up north to live with us would be far better than her being in a home in Surrey. She stayed for over a year before Fran decided that a move to full time residential care was inevitable and could not be delayed any longer. Her sister, Jan, had died a year before Mollie went into the home and Fran carried the burden of making such decisions. When I look back I can see Fran's heartbreak increasingly clearer. She saw her mother's life turned upside down and blown away by this heartless hurricane of an illness.

When I came back from Ireland we were a couple who cared for each other and loved each other. But the days of being in love were no longer tangible and no longer obvious. The number of deaths in our families had taken so much out of us. We held on to each other through each individual suffering, then waited for the next. It was hard to think of the present and impossible to think of the future. When Mollie died I sensed that Fran was running on empty. As usual, she had given everything. I thought I had done the same but looking back, I'm not sure. I made mistakes. Within weeks of her mother dying I encouraged Fran to take a break from work, rest up or perhaps travel. She decided to go part time, working in Leeds Prison. Such work is hard enough at the best of times. It can get you seeing life in blacks and greys, no colour, no smell other than the sweet stench of prison sweat. She never had the break that she needed and I began to think that a new life and a liberation was what she deserved. I never discussed this it at the time. I just encouraged Fran to take time, go away and breathe again. Instead of communicating or showing how I cared in everyday life, I decided to give her space, whatever that means. On painful reflection I think I pushed her away, not deliberately but through a lack of understanding and thought.

Soon she decided to take a break to return to India and retrace her mother and father's journey. Her mother had written a book which traced her and Basil's life in India shortly after the war. Included were the adventures of two young girls, Fran and Jan. The aim was to retrace some of the unforgettable steps of her childhood and to come closer to her parents and sister despite their passing. It was a wonderful idea. She was away for three months and while we both knew that this trip could be life changing for Fran, underneath I'm certain that we knew it would be life changing for our relationship. However, we spoke two or three times each week, often in the early hours, with Fran excitedly reporting on the day's journey and of meetings with those that knew her parents and that knew her as a child. In some ways we started to come a little closer again but I never, for one second, felt that things would be the same again. It was enough for me then and it is enough for me now to know that she was happy and free.

Coming back from India we muddled through. We saw each other as a couple but kept our own independence. Fran had seen that there was another way. For me, I was happy with this. It was almost like waiting for another loss but being more than happy to spend time with someone who I loved despite the loss of being in love. I plodded on, throwing myself more and more into work. I was a Senior Probation Officer at this stage, telling myself that I was enjoying the challenges and responsibilities. Looking back, I now know that I was kidding myself. By Christmas, both Fran and I must have been thinking that this was our last together. We never said as much and when things ended on New Year's Eve, it was almost to be expected. Within three months Fran had sold her house and left the Probation Service. She came to see me to say goodbye. She had found a man who she hoped would be 'her last chance of happiness'. She deserved that. When she left I felt grateful that she had the chance to move on and equally grateful that I had spent so much time with her.

Weeks passed and I started to focus on doing something to spark me up. Work wasn't everything. I needed to refresh myself as well as to let go. Ireland again was the obvious option. I had lifted my spirits so many times in the past year by thinking of that unforgettable time in the Limerick area. I had shown the video shots and shared the tales of the trip with two of my closest friends, Paul and Chris. They agreed that a gentlemen's trip to the area was needed, so we booked a four-day passage. The mere thought of returning there kept me going through spring and into early June. To share the experience with my close friends was an added bonus and an unforgettable one at that.

Paul and I met Chris at Leeds Bradford Airport. For them it was their first trip to Ireland, very much on my recommendation after my short but unforgettable trip the year before. Paul and Chris are very similar in many respects, certainly socially. Both are typically solid Yorkshiremen, enthusiastic Leeds United fans and family men. Both love a good drink and a good bet. Not much different from myself really, hence the suggestion that they see life across the Irish Sea. Also, like myself, they enjoy the craic. I had known Paul over ten years, initially through our regular attendance in a very, very dodgy bookmakers in Cleckheaton. Paul had a love for the dogs and we had bought a few together, including

Daisy, who was now starting her racing career in Sheffield. He had put aside a few days from his hectic business commitments as a wholesale card trader. Likewise, Chris was seeking some 'downtime' from his own exacting duties as a Detective Inspector in the police. That's where we met. No, not in an arrest and charge situation but as colleagues. He was the police representative in managing high risk offenders in what is known as MAPPA, while I played a similar role for the Probation Service. Rightly, we took our duties very seriously. Our mutual multi agency commitments and the demands of working closely with our own service colleagues put a strain on each of us and a few days in Ireland was just the job. Both their wives were, no doubt, glad to let them loose, knowing full well that excessive drinking, gambling and banter would be the only activities that we could sustain at our time in life!

We arrived in Dublin airport in just over forty minutes, soon getting to the pick-up point for the car hire. My old friend Brian Gillard suggested that we head for O'Brien's Bridge, where we could have an initial base for Limerick dog track. Nothing was booked as Brian assured us that wherever we went around O'Brien's Bridge, we'd find all we would need. There was no planned reunion with dear old Larry either. The man who introduced me to the local area in such a short time the year before had passed away with cancer. I had spoken to him a number of times prior to his death as he continued to rear Daisy before her move to England. I was saddened for his passing mainly because this was a man passionate about life, especially his dogs. I could imagine his frustrations knowing that time was running out for himself and his loved ones. As we drove towards Limerick, I spontaneously asked the lads if they didn't mind me stopping off to visit his wife, Babs. However, within a short time I felt slightly uneasy about this, not knowing whether I would be a help or a hindrance. Would my turning up, so soon after his passing, make things harder? On reflection, I took the easy way out for me, falling back on the reserve that living in England often brings and deciding not to visit this time. I learnt in the coming years that the Irish deal with these things, I mean death, a lot better than most of us.

As we made our way down the N7 towards O'Brien's Bridge, Paul and Chris took in the same scenery which caught my eye the year before. On arriving in the village we soon found the Bed and Breakfast recommended by Brian on the Montpelier side of the River Shannon. A lovely lady, Kate, welcomed us warmly, sensing our excitement. Paul had the single room, Chris and myself the double. Paul must have known that he made the right choice as he was guaranteed to get some sleep later on, while Chris and I were destined to stay up too late and drink far too much. Anyway, parked up and booked in, we walked into the Bridge for our first Irish pint. Of course we tried the Guinness and then had a superb fish meal at the Old Mill. It was there that we noticed that there was a rearranged race meeting the following day at Tipperary. That's it, we decided. Tonight Limerick dogs, tomorrow Tipperary races and then the last night in Leopardstown. We were set. Kate gave us the number of someone who would taxi us into town, though he wasn't a taxi driver. We set off and went past what could have been a pub but, equally, could have been someone's front room. From the B and B's window I had noticed a man brushing a wooden floor with Irish music playing as he worked. I asked the driver if it was a pub. "It is and a good one too."

Chris asked, "When does it close?" Which received the reply, "October!" He went on to say that we shouldn't worry too much about opening and closing times. I wish that we knew then what the house-cum-pub would become famous for. A couple of years on, the owner had to consider anything to keep business going. With the economy being increasingly tested, he was in danger of going bust. What else could he do but employ topless bar staff, bringing in a young female to pull the pints and pull the punters in! Nothing new with this back in Yorkshire but in Ireland it made the regional and national news with people visiting from miles away, blocking up the village as trade started to pick up. Unfortunately, the morality of this didn't go down well and after a number of dedicated priests had visited the pub to make their own assessment, the license was withdrawn.

Anyway, we arrived near the Markets Field Greyhound Stadium a shade early. We told the driver not to worry as we would go for a pint across the road. Chris said he felt a shade uncomfortable about this, sensing his Bobbie's instinct. A wall near the pub had a picture of a masked gunman with the Irish Tricolour in the background. The driver said it would be better if we waited in the car with him, indicating that we might be at risk if we wandered into that pub. At that time none of us knew much about the reputation of Limerick City but we were cute enough to listen to advice from a local who clearly didn't want three visitors from the UK wandering blindfold from pub to pub in what might be termed the wrong area...sitting ducks comes to mind!

On entering the stadium and seeing the first dogs with their owners, I quickly thought back to Larry and last year. I had a brief sense of tangible sadness but, somehow, this lifted quickly. It was as though Larry was looking down and saying, "Enjoy yourselves, lads." We did. Paul is a real dog man, the traditional type and he could see the attraction of the stadium with its on-site kennelling, allowing people of all ages to see the dogs prepared and cared for. A few pints later and he was looking for another dog to buy. Impressed by one fast time, he was down from the bar looking for the owner. I suspected that the dog in question would be worth at least a couple of thousand euros, assuming that it was for sale.

"I'll offer three hundred," said Paul, ever the business man looking to pull off a good deal. Tugging at his shirt, I persuaded him not to, otherwise he might be the one running around the track with a fearsome farmer at his heels. I then introduced the lads to Mary Crotty, who remembered me from the previous year when Larry introduced me to the track. As usual she was enthusiastically enjoying a night at the dogs.

We had a great night, no winners but real sport. Our driver arrived to take us back to the village. I think he was relieved to get us out of town in one piece. We were in good spirits. He dropped us at Darby's, a locals bar some thirty yards up from the Old Mill. The Guinness was cold and flowing and the cider likewise. We then made it to the Old Mill for a couple of drinks and sensed that the door was closed for the night despite twenty or so souls drinking beyond closing time. We wouldn't have minded been locked in, that's for sure, but we felt we had better not keep those in the Bed and Breakfast up too late. As we walked the forty yards or so down to the Bridge, there was a sweet stillness in the air, the sort that only seems to be there when you are on holiday in the middle of summer in heavenly surroundings. We started to cross the bridge, three visitors who had a wonderful evening with warm and welcoming people in a beautiful setting. We stopped midway, looking down the River Shannon. Moonlight helped give the water a perfect glaze. It looked like a smooth plate of glass, soundless and motionless. We leaned over the Bridge. I remember saying, "Lads, people actually live here," which Paul and Chris didn't understand at first. What I meant was that for us three, this was a beautiful holiday spot with lovely people and a way of life way beyond our own. We only ever came across such places and experiences a few weeks each year if we were lucky. Yet it was home, everyday home for many lucky souls. Chris and Paul agreed that it would be great to live here but they felt that was unrealistic. Nevertheless, I posed the question, "Why not?"

Since that night the three of us have recalled that conversation many times and they remember that I was beginning to dream about a future in Ireland even then. I know they also recall the end to that night at Kate's B and B. Paul was feeling a bit tired and ropey and declined the chance of a whisky night cap in our room. Unfortunately, Chris didn't have any self-control that night and I never had. We toasted Ireland and a great night many times. The next day the sun beat down on three jolly tourists as we left O'Brien's Bridge behind and set off towards Tipperary. Again, the drive through expensive and lush countryside was awe inspiring. A range of mountains seemed to stretch from one side of the planet to the other. If pretty is a telling word, then it is totally inadequate in describing this landscape. As we drove we sang or we laughed, enjoying the freedom that a good holiday brings. At the end of the journey we came across a superb Bed and Breakfast looking directly on to Tipperary racetrack.

Our hostess was a lively and cheeky landlady, named Angela. She made us feel very welcome in her beautiful home. Before we unpacked, out came quality coffee and homemade biscuits, a refreshing welcome mat typical of the area. She must have sensed pretty early on that this was no ordinary race trip for three middle-aged men in search of entertainment and sport. While Paul and Chris showered and pampered themselves in ready for a night at the races, I took it upon myself to give Angela a form line on both lads. I explained that they were under my professional guidance for the next few days as part of an aftercare programme following their time in rehabilitation units. I had been given the pastoral responsibility for reintegrating these two fallen priests back into the community. I explained, as discreetly as possible, that Father Paul's drinking and gambling had caused his temporary ruination while Father Christy had fallen by the wayside with an over-zealous attraction to ladies of the night. She listened in silence, her mouth widening by the split second. I added that they were good men of God and that their jobs in England were safe, providing they completed this stage of their recovery. I said that their journey back to the Father had been a long one and how they managed the temptations and pressures of the real world was an important part of their recovery. Only then could they be considered men of God again. "God bless you, Terry, you're doing a wonderful job, a wonderful job," she said. The lads came downstairs and Angela wished us well... "Now you boys enjoy yourselves at the races but go steady now so."

Paul and Chris, in pure oblivion to my disclosure, commented on her lovely warmth and hospitality. We then had a great night at the races at Tipperary's beautiful provincial track with the most stunning backdrop of scenery you will see for the price of a race ticket. This was sport at its best without the over commercialised influences which seep into horseracing these days. Keiran Fallon's comeback from suspension was the sporting highlight and also the human highlight. This man is the villain of the peace in some quarters and the devil's naked whip on a horse. He is also an inspired genius and as humanly faulted as the rest of us. This and his genius and ferocious drive in the saddle makes him a loved one for many. When he drove the Bogberry late and fast to the winning line, he was destined to get a rousing welcome from his fans in the winner's enclosure.

Then from the sublime to the ridiculous as Paul put it…the sight of an intoxicated priest, whisky in one hand, crumbling ciggy in the other, wandering between the bookmakers for the best odds!

"Would you give me evens the top one?"

"We would, Father, and you can have the best odds if it goes out." I wondered if I had dressed my two 'fallen priests' up in their clerical uniform, would we have had better odds on Fallon's mount?

Well-oiled and merry, we went to the Pub across the road from the track for a night cap or two. Highlights of Hurling caught Paul and Chris's eye as they tried to see 'the ball', the sliotar, as the Hurleys flashed and crashed in mid-air, parting hair through the player's helmets. I doubt whether they could see the sport in this, either drunk or sober. Nevertheless, we set off to Angela's and I told the lads that they should behave like sober gentlemen, given that Angela told me that she thought they were priests on holiday. They cursed me, "You're joking, you are joking…she thought we were men of the cloth and you told her we were priests on holiday?" I admitted to this but only told the full story when we had set off to Leopardstown the next day.

Before we left the next morning, I signed the visitor's book on behalf of the two priest's in my care but did not tell them until we were twenty miles down the road. They cursed me like two good priests should and promised to gain due revenge. And they did. Within an hour of our journey they dropped me outside a newsagent, where the Racing Post was the sole requirement. Again the shopkeeper showed that warmth and humour, which I was beginning to find so typical of the trip. As I left the shop, half an eye on my Racing Post and half an eye on the oncoming traffic, I slipped into the back seat. I glanced at the shop window to see three faces pressed against the glass, lips moving in turn, each obviously making a comment. Within seconds a car pulled alongside. Chris looked across and opened the window… "What are you doing in there, mate?"

I knew straightaway that I'd got into the wrong car and immediately went to the shop to explain myself. They readily accepted my explanation, laughed me out of the shop and wished me all the best for Leopardstown. Paul and Chris were still in fits of laughter, having seen me enter a local's car and settle down for the ride! They'd seen it coming and were happy enough to see me get close to being arrested for simply being thoughtless. Still, the locals saw the funny side and we set off for our final night at Leopardstown races. The night passed like the rest of the trip, the highlights being an 8/1 winner in the big handicap which we all had, plus quality racing and general entertainment. Somehow we ended up in the members bar for well over an hour and we couldn't believe the sensitive and understanding way that staff let us know that we were out of bounds. They were courteous and very polite. We drank too much to remember how we ended up drinking alongside trainers, jockeys and journalists. Nevertheless, we hadn't drunk too much to forget how well we were treated. No fuss, no snobbery, just everyone intent on having a good time and behaving. That perhaps summed up the trip for all of us. Unforgettable people, so relaxed, buckets of fun and craic. Add to that, great sport, immeasurable hospitality and constantly beautiful settings. This was an experience we would never forget. As we left for the airport the next day, I told the lads that I would be back and that one day it would be for good. I bought a paper to look at the mundane things in life such as job vacancies, rental and housing prices and as I scanned through, translating euros into pounds, I hoped this wouldn't be a futile exercise.

# 3 – The Turning Point

In the next two years I returned to Ireland a couple of times with Chris and other friends. Chris also returned with his wife Liz and their two sons. He stayed a night at Angela's in Tipperary, who, no doubt, recognised him as Father Christy, the delinquent priest with an appetite for ladies of the night! What she made of Father Christy's family I'll never know. As for myself, each trip reignited the dream of moving to Ireland, but, for now, this was all it could be. Mum was still her spirited self and getting by, despite her failing health. Daisy was also getting by and she filled our hearts with many a wonderful moment. She went through the grades, A7 to A3 at Sheffield, winning in her grade and always running to her name, Calon Lan i.e., Pure Heart. Though I joined a web site for jobs in Ireland, I would never leave the UK while Mum was alive. For the present we had the dogs to keep us happy and entertained and any dreams of a life elsewhere could wait.

I'd had a taste of a new world but had settled back into the old world, often happy enough but with no view to the future. Looking back I think I was hiding a truth or two. I had good friends in Yorkshire and a good job with a purpose. Yet I was very, very unsettled. I had put my relationship with Fran in a cupboard, closed the draw and conveniently forgotten it. I had the odd liaison but never pursued any relationship with commitment or intent for the future. I was more than happy to be alone with my retired greyhounds. Connie, Flossie, Ollie and Bart were all at home at one stage. They were my family, having all burst a gut on the track before coming home to a life of pipe and slippers, chicken and curry. I had some contact with Ronnie's boys but they were big enough and ugly enough to get into trouble and romance without their uncle. Life was Sky Sports TV, occasional nights at the dogs and a bit too much drinking at home. In a way I felt that this was it, make the most of it and enjoy the choices that you make when you can.

At this stage greyhound racing and the retired heroes were my life as were they Mum's. They certainly kept Mum going. From the early days of Connie, right through to Daisy, Mum and I had glorious days and some very sad nights. Winning always resulted in me ringing her in North Wales to say, "Well done, owner," and then discuss the race many times over. A good run from one of our dogs and even better, a win, would lift Mum's spirits enormously. Excited isn't the word, passionate neither. Their runs, their wins, the prospects for any new pup we had, it all provided the richest blood line to her heart. Even sad nights when a dog would be injured, only broke our hearts for a while, though some more than others. We had many dogs, owned in partnership with my mate Paul, and while some had career ending injuries on the track, all survived to have long and happy retirements. Daisy included. She sits behind me in the chair, right now, keeping my back warm and my heart warmer. Daisy raced fifty-one times. On the last occasion we received a call from the track at Sheffield from Jane Houfton, the trainer. Daisy had broken her leg, a very bad break and it was unlikely that she would survive. I trusted Jane so much and asked if there was a chance at all that Daisy could be saved or, alternatively, whether it was right to stop the suffering there and then. Jane felt that she had a chance. She and her team had come to love Daisy and she would have known the value to our own hearts to have her home. Thankfully, after an operation she survived and came home. Mum was so relieved. Daisy's injury nearly broke her heart that night.

Mum continued to visit two or three times a year...not so much to see me but to see the dogs! The times we had are stained in my memory in beautiful colours and in totally clear sound. I recall her vividly talking to each and every dog and I recall even more clearly how each dog lovingly talked to her. They ran for Mum. They had done so ever since Connie's early days when the legendary Harry Crapper had her in his care. He is the greatest trainer never to have won the English Derby, in my opinion, having gone so, so close on two occasions. What's more, he certainly is the gentleman of the sport, ever courteous and considerate and like Jane Houfton, Daisy's trainer, someone who knew how much these dogs meant to my mother.

Yet things changed in the autumn of 2007. Mum became ill with a breathing problem. She had to go into hospital in St Asaph but within five days they had her stabilised and she was told she would be going home at the weekend. Unfortunately, though, within the next day or so she caught an infection and within a few short hours was confined to a room of her own with salmonella. A liver infection developed. The family in North Wales visited non-stop and I travelled down regularly from Yorkshire on the train. These were journeys in darkness as I dreaded what I would see and what I would hear. I felt like a boy of eight but as vulnerable as a child of two. I spoke to a consultant who warned me of the worst. I began to realise where my heart was or rather where it should be. As Mum began to miraculously fight back, I was looking forward. I made a decision that I needed to change things before it was too late. To return home to Wales, spend more time with Mum and the family and get away from the rat race.

With God's help, the family's strength and Mum's typical courage, she recovered to the extent that they decided to send her home for Xmas. The Friday before Xmas eve I set off back to Denbigh. Mum was being released from hospital that day and I would be with her for the fortnight to make sure she settled in OK. The week before, my mind made up, I told my boss, Neil Moloney, that I would be living in Wales by the start of April the following year. He had ample time to come to terms with my plans and understood my reasoning totally. That helped. My decision had been easy to make in the end but the process needed some ploughing through. I was jaded, tired, scared and very unsure of the future. Mum's illness made me realise that the worst moment of my life was in the future, sometime, if not very soon.

For years I had known that Mum's death would break my heart. We'd been through so many good times and shared so many bad times. The latter are the hardest to consider, to recollect, but during her illness all my memories and fears came out. The person who loved and nurtured me into a reasonable human being was close to the end. As a child I knew what Mum went through with my father. He was a violent alcoholic, always handy to intimidate and raise a fist to my mum. She tried to escape by taking me to Yorkshire to live with Aunty Beryl and Uncle Ron. He chased us down. The rest was predictable. He spent the following years trying to dominate and control his wife through domestic violence. We survived together. When I was old enough to take him on, I at least felt that I could try and protect Mum. We looked after each other, shared the misery of sharing a house but never a home. I grew up seeing how loving, brave and committed one parent could be and how cowardly and destructive another could be. Those days bonded us and made me.

The older I got, the more I became proud of my mother. The more I began to appreciate her sacrifices to give her son a good start in life. Despite the lack of money or security and despite too many miserable days, she did this. When I was sixteen, Mum suffered a brain haemorrhage and Doctor Hyland believed domestic violence could have contributed to this. On the night of the operation to save her life, Dad and I fought in a bedroom, the blood splattering in slow motion over the white quilt Mum had bought only days before. When I pushed his drunken, smelly body away, he promised he would change. But nothing did. From the day Mum came home from hospital, bald, scarred and with her skull indented, to the day he died, my father was never a man to my mother.

When Mum reached sixty, my sister Amanda and I schemed to help her escape. Before she retired I went with her to see a solicitor. He asked for examples of unreasonable behaviour, ten if possible. I'll never forget Mum freezing, being unable to answer. She was paralysed by the fear of taking Dad on and finding her freedom. I helped her by recalling examples of his behaviour. We walked out of the solicitor's office, knowing that the first steps to her safe and free future had been made. I told her that if she did not see this through, he would kill her with intent or not.

The divorce came through when she was in South Africa visiting Auntie Beryl. Dad never believed it would happen and he still believed she would come back, despite me making it clear that there was no chance of this. When Mum came back from South Africa, she moved straight to Amanda and John's in North Wales. John then found her a flat to rent. She was physically free. Before she moved to the flat, the old man went looking for her. He came up against a brick wall. While Mum was with my sister Amanda and John he had no chance of harming her. John is the best brother-in-law I could have wished for. Protective to his family, she was in safe hands. And when my father returned to Yorkshire I told him that if he ever wanted to see me again, he must never chase down Mum again. It was an ultimatum. Mum insisted that I didn't walk away from him, despite everything he did to her and the fights we had. Thankfully, Dad respected the way forward and it was the start of many years when he learnt to live independently.

Mum had twenty-five years of freedom in North Wales and we visited each other frequently. She was home now, living in Denbigh, so close to the village of Trefnant where the family grew up. Her brothers, Ken and Derek, were all nearby with the extended family. Amanda and John lived close to Mum and with their children, Nicola and Paul, they provided 25 years of family life for Mum which I knew she cherished. When her grandchildren married and brought her first great grandchildren, Mum's life had been completed. Compared to those dark, dark days with my father, her retirement years back home in Wales were unbelievably warm and loving. Yet I knew that one day they would end and my visit to stay with Mum in that Xmas of 2007 would prove to be pivotal in my life.

I was down there to look after Mum with the family. As usual John and Amanda were brilliant and as usual Nic and Paul were loving grandchildren, adults now and coping with the possibility of their very first deep loss. Within hours of being home I knew Mum was not herself. She was confused, exhausted and could hardly walk. The day after she was home we took her back in to hospital again with pain in her leg. They released her that night, saying it was a trapped nerve. On Christmas Day she was again in pain. She was too unsettled to go to Nicola's for Christmas dinner and so we stayed in together watching TV. Those were the last hours that I spent with Mum at home. It broke my heart to see her in increasing pain and I had to call an ambulance. At the hospital they settled her down for the night and she was safe and in good hands. We went home, fearing the worst but not knowing the worst. It took a couple of days for essential tests to be completed. Then Amanda received a call asking both of us to go in to see the Consultant.

We went in and waited to see the consultant, in fear, expecting the worst. Mum's leg had lost blood supply and she had developed septicaemia. She had a ten-percent chance of survival but only if they fully amputated her leg. There were no guarantees and no odds in our favour. We looked at each other and shook our heads. We did not need to discuss anything in terms of whether to take this very slim, cruel chance. This very slim chance which would prolong the suffering of our lovely mum. All that needed to be discussed was how her life should end. Nothing else mattered other than this. They promised a private room as soon as we left as they said she may die within days.

We came back three hours later after ringing and telling the rest of the family. They arranged times to visit and to say goodbye. Paul, her beloved grandson, was understandably anxious not to visit, wanting to remember his Gran in better days. By 8 p.m. most of the family had come and gone. I said I would stay. I needed to be there for myself as much as for Mum. She had always been there for me. The night passed. Mum was occasionally distressed and I asked for more medication. The nursing staff were good and considerate, not least Nicola's best friend, Leah, who nursed there. She came to check on me, reassure me, almost like an angel. I had seen my brother Ronnie and my father both pass away in a local hospice in Yorkshire. This was different. The biggest and best part of my heart and character was going with Mum's passing. Yet I managed to focus on holding her hand and talked about the good times. She couldn't speak as she was very tired, but she occasionally squeezed my hand to reply to a question.

Mum survived the night, though every now and again I sensed her leaving as breathing patterns changed. The next day John and Amanda came back. My brave nephew, Paul, and my loving niece, Nicola, arrived. I am certain Mum waited for them. Certain. Absolutely certain. John and Amanda then went home just before Coronation Street started. I talked to Mum again. "Mum, haven't we had some dogs? Sometimes I can't remember them all." I then recited them in order or at least I tried to. Mum squeezed my hand very gently, very tiredly, a few times.

"We need to get another, Mum, what do you reckon? What about another bitch? We could call her Trefnant

Girl…what do you think?" She squeezed my hand very gently. Then she didn't squeeze again. Not long after this, her breathing changed and I sensed she was going. I turned to find a Nurse. Leah entered the room by chance, there and then. She said Mum was going but was still with us and she could hear me. I said goodbye, gave my love and my everlasting thanks. Time stood still but didn't. My heart stopped but didn't.

# 4 – Going Home to Wales

The month before Mum passed away that Xmas, I had promised myself that I would move to North Wales before the end of the following March. The house was on the market, work had been given notice of my plans and I was determined to find a new life. Mum's suffering and eventual death focused me on my own mortality and the need to consider what I wanted in the time that lay ahead. My plan to be in North Wales before April would coincide with my fiftieth birthday. For all the experiences growing up as a Yorkshire Welshman, I had had enough of concrete and the hectic pace of life, typical of urban West Yorkshire. Consequently, I returned to Liversedge after the funeral intent on finishing off my professional responsibilities and finalising plans for the move. At the funeral my heart had almost cracked like frozen brittle glass. I didn't feel the healthiest, physically or emotionally, and I knew that if I didn't escape to a rural world, I would die in Yorkshire like Dad and Brother Ronnie. It would have been easier to change my mind, stick with comforts and routines. But, from somewhere, my plan to move home and make a fresh start was reignited. Little did I know that this was to be one step over a stream with another leap over a river in the distance.

By mid-March I had secured work in Wrexham in the Council's Social Services team, courtesy of their manager, David O'Brien. Now I could focus on the last few weeks closing the books on my work and life in Yorkshire and saying goodbye to friends and Ronnie's boys. I wanted things to finish pretty quickly at the end. The plan was to finish at work on the Friday, have my leaving 'do' that night and set off to North Wales the next morning. It just so happened that it was my birthday that weekend, so I had a roller coaster of a few days before starting work in Wrexham on the Wednesday. My last day in the Probation Service in Bradford was a great day for me but it tested my emotions. It was only right to give heartfelt thanks to all those who I had known in over seventeen years. I was so proud of what we had achieved in public service, so grateful to have known so many good people. My mate, Chris, turned up and many ghosts from my professional past. The Probation Service had given me so much, not least the chance to do something constructive with my life. It had given me the chance to work with so many very good people. People who were professional and caring.

Yes, it was only right to celebrate the end of my Yorkshire life with many friends and colleagues who meant so much to me. Of course, Chris and Paul were there, plus Henryk. He was a friend before my probation days and throughout them. As good a colleague as you would want and a great man for partying. A rock solid friend who would give you an honest answer to an honest question. Though Henryk has a serious side to him, he would never take himself too seriously. He professed to being an expert in relationship counselling and he would always be happy to share his worldly-wise advice over a drink or two. Many a good man would ring him for

44

advice when the embers of the heart went cold, including myself and many other probation officers. Our old friend, Seb, the ever romantic Dom, the liberally romantic Fitzy and the incorrigible rogue called Robbo. In need of wisdom we all went to the font of all sensitive knowledge, our friend Henryk. Yes, without doubt he is a legend in counselling the affairs of the heart…though in all those years that he counselled his friends, often diligently into the early hours, whisky frequently to everyone's lips, nobody can ever recall the advice he gave. Nor can he.

Also on the coach was dear old Bungalow. I'll not embarrass him by giving his real name but the Bungalow was aptly named. Nothing up top but everything where it mattered. We'd been good friends a long time. I am one of a small group of friends, plus all those dozens who performed with him, plus the cameramen who knew of his former life. From European porn star to West Yorkshire plumber, Bungalow imported his porn star moustache to Leeds, bringing with him a bag of tools which always made him popular with the ladies. He advertised himself simply as 'The Repair Man' and there is no doubt he could turn his hand to anything in his specialist field.

Anyway, we went off to the dogs, a coachload of fifty-seven. Someone had contacted Jane, the trainer, to enter my and Mum's remaining dog, Alchemist Wish. You can guess that fairy tales still happen and, of course, 'Wish' bolted in. I went to collect the trophy as the whole group sang and shouted. I will never forget that. We all tried to get in the photograph as an expertly dressed gentleman flashed away with his camera. "I am the photographer for the night," he said to three of the younger women. "But you can call me the pornographer!" Needless to say we had a merry old journey home with whisky and beer being passed around to those with room for more. Chris tried to entice me to stay out for longer, starting in some karaoke bar in Bradford. A rendition of 'What's New Pussycat?' would have gone down well or maybe the 'Green, green grass of home'. I was tempted but needed at least a few hours sleep before my repatriation to Wales.

Despite our excesses the night before, Paul and I set off for Wales at eight o'clock the next day. After just a couple of days to settle the dogs in, I started working in Wrexham on a sessional basis for three days a week. It paid the bills and gave me the chance to start developing a balanced lifestyle, giving me time in my homeland with my family. They were as caring and helpful as ever. Friday evenings were something I came to love, 6 p.m. around at my sister's for a couple of hours before setting off back home to watch rugby league. Growing up for over 45 years away from my sister had limited my time with her to holidays, visits, Xmas and the rest. I'd always made the most of my visits to North Wales with Amanda and John and their 'kids', Nicola and Paul. They had their own families now and it was great to be close and part of the family. The dogs settled well and had the benefit of wonderful country walks. I settled well too. I knew within weeks that I had made the right decision. I knew that I would never go back to an urban environment and I was now certain that I needed to get a good balance between work and the rest of my life.

Yet work was a challenge in the Wrexham Learning Disability Team, the hardest job I had taken on. There was very little client contact. My job was to help win resources from the Health Service over to the Local Authority. After a few months I was getting the hang of it. However, if truth were known, I was a fish out of water, totally at times. Spreadsheets and case management budgets were OK for social workers, I guess, but not for a probation officer. I realised that I needed to get back into probation if possible before I got rumbled. Before people found out that my heart wasn't in it. Only the pay, part time work and wonderful colleagues got me by. Plus, of course the regular two bottles of red on a Friday, one at John and Amanda's, one back at home watching the Rugby. In fact it was the red wine and the Friday night ritual that collided together to turn my new world upside down.

It must have been early June 2008, only three months after moving to Denbigh. I'd wandered around to John and Amanda's. We had the usual banter and chat. I loved those nights. John was a bugger. I always used to get there and think I'll have just a couple but his company and tales have always made me drink more! Anyway, a bit later than usual I set off home, let the dogs out and settled for the evening. This obviously entailed further wine tasting, an art encouraged over the years by my good mate, Henryk in Yorkshire. By ten o'clock I had the choice between bed or the computer, trying to catch up on e-mails. I chose the latter, knowing full well that it had been a good week since I'd 'spoken' to friends. I'd also, sporadically, opened a job vacancy site for Ireland, which I had signed up to ever since I bought the computer. During this time I'd opened the front page mail many, many times, maybe hundreds of times. While Mum had been alive it was something just to look at to consider. Since her death some six months earlier it was just the same, though most of the e mails notifying me of a job in the public sector had never been opened. I had no interest in anything at this time other than settling with my family. This was my future. I needed to be there.

Yet this night was different. I opened the e-mails one by one, ignoring a few on the way. In time I reached the familiar heading for jobs in Ireland. For whatever reason I will never know, I stopped as if being shot. In recent months I had not even bothered to open the site, assuming it was another job for the Gardai or Fisheries etc. But on this unique occasion something had wrestled my drunken attention even before the site was opened. In a reflex moment, I turned to the dogs, all legged out in comfort. Before opening that particular e mail, that particular job site, I said, "Hey up, girls, this is the probation job, this is the Irish probation job." Why I sensed that I will never, ever know. I pressed the key and entered the site to see that it was for the national recruitment of probation officers in the Republic of Ireland. I know my heart nearly stopped, spooked by this very, very odd, split second prediction and the result on the screen. My world went still, there and then, almost frozen as I looked at the dogs. I sobered up immediately. What did this mean? I managed to sleep but woke up wondering what does this mean, if anything at all. I will never be able to explain what happened that night but I'm glad there were three retired greyhounds to witness it!

I rang Paul and Chris the next day. I expected them to laugh, not to believe me, to simply give a blunt Yorkshire response. Something like "ah, ya, soft bugger, cut down on the booze". Or maybe "you've made enough changes, just settle with your family now and enjoy yourself". But they didn't. I thought I knew them. I was the dreamer, not them. Yet they both said, more or less, exactly the same.

"You've got to go for it…remember how much you've loved Ireland. There's nothing to stop you going for it." Looking back, I still can't believe their response as it was so out of character. I decided two things there and then. I would apply for the job. But I would not tell my family. The chances of me getting an interview were very slim. Given my location and the fact that I had worked as a Team Manager for the past six-and-a-half years and would be ring rusty as main grade probation officer, I felt I had no real chance, so there was no point in unsettling the family.

I received the application form and thought that I'd apply as much in response to the events of that spooky Friday night as in response to my previous dreams of living in Ireland. I had nothing to lose except a couple of hours filling in a job application. The encouragement to apply from Chris and Paul was the final push. Some weeks later I received a letter offering an interview. Again I was shocked and I again rang my mates. They both thought it was comical and said that I would have to see it through, go for the interview and let 'what will be, will be'. I agreed, drank some more red and booked return flights to Dublin. My family were used to me going in recent years and I said it was for a long weekend, Thursday night at Leopardstown races and Friday at Harold's Cross dogs…and so it was.

On getting to Dublin, I booked into the hotel near Leopardstown races before having a steady night punting. I didn't have an early night, considering I had an interview the next day. I simply made the most of the trip with low expectations of any job prospects but intent on enjoying

Ireland once again. The next day I made my way to Dublin city centre and turned up for the interview. There was another candidate in the waiting room. He said that we were the last two. I asked if they had been interviewing all day. He chuckled, saying that they had been interviewing for the past two weeks for 10 to 12 positions! Right there and then, I just felt great relief as I knew that I had no chance, especially when he said there had been one hundred and forty who made the interview stage!

I recall the interview well, not least the questions like "Why the Probation Service again and why Ireland?" I decided that it would have been rude to say, "For the craic, the drinking and gambling." but the eagle eyed bearded manager on the far left saw right into my soul and wanted an honest answer. I cited my growing affection for the country after recent visits, plus the opportunity to build on my past experiences and face another challenge. I was honest in saying it was as much a lifestyle move as a professional challenge. They gave me a fair hearing and in thanking them for that opportunity I said goodbye to them and my dream.

That night I enjoyed Harold's Cross dogs and felt so, so happy that I had achieved my dream simply by pursuing it. I was proud of that and the fact that I at least tried. I did have some regret, however, that my chance would never come again. But, at least I tried and I had left the interview knowing that my new life in my homeland with my family would be a lasting and priceless consolation. The next day I arrived home, never a word about the interview, my secret hidden forever.

However, about four weeks later I received a phone call from Dublin, advising me that the interview panel's decision had been formally relayed to the Irish Probation Service website. I thought this was an unusual way of releasing results of a job interview. However, I opened up the site, wondering why they had rang me. It opened up and led to a box which said, "Your position in the panel is…One…" I know my heart stopped then, I simply know it did. It was daytime, I wasn't drunk but I couldn't understand what was going on. "Your position in the panel is one." I rang Dublin back and simply asked, "What does this mean?" The woman must have thought that I was very slow. Yes, she confirmed, this was the interview result and yes, I would be offered a job. She added that because I was number one in the panel, I would automatically get first call…that my choice to work in Limerick would be met. I thanked her and thanked her. I sat down and consulted with the dogs. I told them that 'the Irish job' was on if I wanted it. Me out of one hundred and forty people interviewed, having the first choice to work in Limerick. They didn't believe it either. Flossie looked at me with those olive-coloured eyes as if to say, "Been drinking again, Dad?" The dogs were no use in helping me make sense of this so I rang the lady in Dublin back. I apologised for bothering her and asked again:

"Does this definitely mean I will be offered a job?" On receiving the 'yes' I asked if it definitely will be Limerick, given my position on the panel. 'Yes'. I thanked her for what seemed like the one thousandth time. I sat down and time sat down with me. What does this really mean? Is the dream really on? How the hell could I have done it? How could I have finished first in the panel? Who took my place in the interview? What would Mum say? She must have known, must have had a word with God and asked Him to do me a favour. This was one of those moments in life when I was certain that other forces influenced my life, maybe controlled my life. (Though two years later I heard a rumour that I was placed 1$^{st}$ in the panel to ensure I was available to eventually take up a much dreaded job in the prison, which no alert Irish officer wanted!)

That night I rang Paul and Chris and asked their advice. I thought they'd say 'think on it' but they said I had to go, it was meant to be. I started to think it might well be fate or God's decree or part of another plan. I knew that I never, ever deserved a chance like this. I went around to John and Amanda's shell shocked but silent about my secret news. I decided to enjoy the night and deal with the future the next day. Throughout the early evening, however, I sensed my own dishonesty, my failure to tell them of my interview and my dreams. I also sensed that I would lose precious time with my family if I went. Yet, more than anything else, I felt that this opportunity was not for me to decline. I didn't sleep much that night, despite the red wine. I tossed and turned, pondering over when and how I would tell them, the close and loving family who had done everything to welcome me and help me settle back home. Here I was, only a few short and sweet months back in my home of heritage, a Welshman sounding like a Yorkshireman and looking over to Ireland for my future.

On waking the next day I checked the e-mail and the Probation site to check I wasn't dreaming. Right. That was it. I was going. The rest of the weekend I considered how I would give the news to my Denbigh family and tried to guess their reaction. The most important thing was the fact that they were strong despite Mum's passing. They were so close, so positive and I knew that they would be fine wherever I was. I also knew in my heart of hearts that when the news was out they would understand, sooner or later. They had always been that way. When my engagement broke off from Karen, a month before the wedding, they understood and supported me. Likewise, with Fran, they never bothered my conscience, respecting my choice to live my life. My only real doubt was the impact of Mum's passing, no more than six months earlier. Yet their love of her and family life had made them very strong. I knew that weekend that when I eventually left for Ireland, I would be the weak one, not them.

I waited for the written job offer, subject to all the security checks. When it arrived I went to see John and Amanda and belatedly told the truth. John was John. Solid, listening, taking it in. A good man. He never judged me when I told them, nor since. Amanda seemed to be more shocked and, typical of my lovely sister, she was immediately thinking of the possible negative consequences for myself. They seemed to understand why the interview had been a secret. They seemed to understand all the time. I felt I had betrayed their love and support by going, yet I knew it had to be. I needed full time work, permanent work and it had to be a job I could do. They understood that. We didn't talk too much about my dream at this point. It was wrong too. Sometimes sharing a dream can break a heart. It was something for another day. For now, Ireland was a full time job, good pay and 'something I'd always fancied'. Mum knew that. When I told John and Amanda of my decision, something or somebody helped me. I think I know who.

The next day Nicola and Paul spoke to me. They appeared to understand but I sensed they weren't the happiest. That was understandable. They never said anything to that effect but we often talked over the years about me coming home to Wales. Now it had happened, I was now off. In the coming weeks Paul and Amanda both suggested other jobs. If I could find something permanent, why go? Though I had accepted the Limerick job, I kept an open mind but knew full well that God's will would happen. I wanted to face the challenge of a different world, one that I had fallen in love with in recent years. Yet Wales and family was home. I also had Ronnie's boys on my mind. But I always felt they were strong together, close enough to look after each other in difficult times.

Anyway, the clock kept ticking. I put things down to fate, God's will, call it what you want. I decided to make firm plans and yet I applied for a rare job, the MAPPA Co-ordinator for North Wales…basically the exact same responsibilities that I had in West Yorkshire before I moved to Denbigh. Nephew Paul saw the job, an important job which would give me the responsibility to play a key role in public protection in North Wales. Was this what was meant to be after all? Was Ireland a dream and only that? I had a few words with the Good Lord and then decided to put an application in. If I got an interview that would be one thing. I would give it my best shot and leave it in the lap of God. If I was then offered the job I would have a problem. My heart said that Ireland was a dream that you only see rarely, maybe once in a lifetime. My head said that a greater force would influence events and decide. All I should do was play my cards cleanly and openly and await the outcome.

So I applied for the job only to find that I got an interview. Nephew Paul and Cheryl helped with the technical aspects of the power point as I prepared for the rest of the assessment process. I did my best as I promised myself I would do but the officer acting up in the post got the job. My disappointment was only in that I lost in a competition. My relief was that I did not have to go through days of dilemma – should I stay, should I go? My happiness was that the dream was meant to be. I was not sure if God made the call or whether Mum had a word with him or maybe a bit of both. Not sure if I underperformed in the interview and not sure if I simply wasn't good enough or whether it was a bit of both. Uncertainty can bother us all, but on this occasion I did not give a damn. That night I went to John and Amanda's and simply said, "That's it, I'm going." As supportive and practical as ever, we started to discuss plans.

My old mate, Brian Gillard, was delighted to hear my call the next day. I had made enquiries with a number of agents for properties to rent with kennels for the dogs. So far, not so good and I would never leave Ollie and Daisy behind. Never. Connie had died in Yorkshire and taken a big chunk of my heart with her. Flossie had died in recent weeks and again walked away with part of me. All the dogs had been with me through every emotion in recent years and they had helped me through. Ollie would have to come because she was the Dream of Olwen, who meant so much to Mum and I needed her there for my dream…and, of course, this was all because of Daisy. Without my first ever Irish adventure to see Daisy the pup and to share time with Larry in his very special country, none of this would have been happening.

But it was happening. I needed to be in work on November 27th, 2008. Brian offered to pick me up in North Wales and take me there with the odd bag of clothes, a couple of suits and two greyhounds. But where to? He rang Mary

Crotty in O'Brien's Bridge, explaining that I would welcome any ideas, any local contacts. I called her the next day and she told me that finding rented property with space for greyhounds was not easy. However, she suggested that I get a local B and B and put the dogs in kennels so that I had time to get started at work and search for the right property. She then rang back to give the names of three sisters in the village who did Bed and Breakfast. One was Kate, who accommodated Paul, Chris and myself those few years earlier. Mary also said that she and her husband, John, would kennel the dogs while I settled in. Unbelievable. My starting point in Ireland, even for just a few days, would be in O'Brien's Bridge, providing Kate would agree to take me in. And she did. I went to sleep that night, wondering how and why things were falling in to place. Wondering why people were so good to me, so helpful...wondering once again for the umpteenth time whether all this adventure from dream to reality was just that. Was this real and if so, why?

So that was it. I made the final arrangements in the next two weeks. I left Wrexham Learning Disability team after the manager, Dave O'Brien, offered to make my job permanent. I then took the final steps to say 'goodbye' to my family. A lot had happened in the past year. Mum's illness and passing, turning my back on my beloved Yorkshire friends and Ronnie's boys and now leaving my Welsh family. Throughout it all, someone was looking out for me.

# 5 – Ireland Beckons

On November 24, my old mate, Brian Gillard, drove from Yorkshire to Denbigh, from where we set off to O'Brien's Bridge in County Clare. On locking the house door behind me, I wondered when I would be back. It was only a flash thought, then a flash answer. Did it matter? Of course not but this time I wasn't going on any old holiday, I was leaving for a new life, new job and all. The good thing about going to Ireland with Brian is that he'd never give you the chance to be sentimental. He's as solid as the darkest Yorkshire coal with blunt sides and few sharp edges. We settled down to the drive to Holyhead, listening to Brian's old comedy tapes as he chuckled away beneath his thick moustache and brown glasses. My main worry was how the dogs would manage the ferry but Brian wasn't bothered. So practical compared to me. Anyway, the one way ticket to Ireland continued, crossing Anglesey, where my mother's family came from. My mind wandered as we passed a redundant train station, heading towards Holyhead. I wondered whether this was the setting where my great grandfather worked and lived as the village station master before he headed to east Wales to start his own new adventures in Rhewl. Here I was admiring his beautiful back garden, edged by miles and square miles of harsh moorland and fields. Here I was, some one hundred and twenty years later, heading in the opposite direction in search of my own dreams.

At the ferry I expected someone to check the car, certainly check the dog's identity. Quite the opposite. "You've got dogs? We'll not disturb them." I liked that, though I shouldn't have been surprised given the thousands that bounce around between the countries each year. But for this one day, it was just these two dogs that mattered. Dream of Olwen, Ollie, making her first journey from her Yorkshire home and Calon Lan, Daisy, making her way home to where my adventures all started. A nice thought which I kept to myself. Any 'soft talk' would have got Brian saying, "Ya, big soft bugger." Still I know that even his emotions raised and swam with the tide whenever he went to Ireland. He lived there in Wexford before he and Jackie went back to England, leaving many Irish friends behind. My trip over was also his excuse, if he ever needed one, to come and see some pups to buy. Perfect.

Landing in Dublin, we were soon heading down the N7. As Brian listened to further tapes, I took in the view, beginning to wonder how the next few days would go. I only had three days to settle the dogs at John and Mary's, settle myself in the B and B and get ready for work on the Thursday. I decided there and then as we flew through the vast spaces of sculptured race land called the Curragh that I needed to employ some of Brian's very focused mind set. There was an awful lot to sort in the practical sense and the dreamer in me needed to be put on the back burner. If I got off on the wrong foot, made the wrong decisions and upset the wrong people, I'd be on my way back before I'd started! There was plenty of time to enjoy my new homeland but I needed to focus for now.

Saying all that, as we journeyed west towards Limerick my spirits lifted and started itching, giving me the same nervous edge of excitement that I had when I first came to the area. O'Brien's Bridge came in sight as we turned off from Birdhill. I sensed my eyes widening, taking in the panoramic view. I knew then as if I ever needed to be reminded why I was here. I remember that return to the Bridge as though it is happening now, clear and enticing.

We off loaded at Kate's B and B. My few possessions, just all I needed to start a new life…two suits, a large bag of clothes and the brief case Mum had bought when I set out on my career. Plus a few personal belongings, of course. Pictures of every dog and the family. My leaving card and a few momentos from the Probation Service. My Bible given to me by Dorothy all those years ago in 1988 on leaving the Reach Project. I'm not a great Bible reader but it's often the first place that I look when I need some clarity, need some help. And of course, the two dogs. How many people emigrate with two greyhounds in tow, I don't know. But they were always to start the dream even if we would never all see it through.

Once I'd dropped my kit off, we drove over the bridge linking the two small villages, Montpelier and O'Brien's Bridge. It straddles over the Shannon in the most picturesque and refreshing setting you could imagine. Following the road around to the left, passing Bonners and 'The Old Mill', we arrived at Inislosky Kennels within a minute. Brian knew Mr and Mrs John Crotty from before as Mary had reared a number of pups for him in the past. For me it was good to see a friendly and welcoming face in Mary, the third time we'd met, the first away from the greyhound track. Kitted in her usual comfortable attire of loose bottoms, sweatshirt and wellies, she advertised her role perfectly. Country woman, practical, happy to graft hard and muck in. No airs and graces about Mary but a lovely, genuine warmth, nonetheless. She introduced her husband, John, a spritely, healthy looking man, hardly carrying an ounce of fat. His physique told the tale that he was a working man. As we talked over tea in their kitchen, Daisy and Ollie were in one of their paddocks, letting off steam. Within seconds I could see they were enjoying themselves in their new surroundings, tails wagging and eyes peeled back like seals in a documentary film. While they had fun, the grown-ups talked, mainly about my plans. At this stage they were happy to look after the dogs while I was over at Kate's and while I searched for accommodation and settled into work. From the first minute John and Mary took a weight off my mind, ever helpful and reassuring.

However, even in our early conversations around the table where I have since spent many happy hours, I realised that I would soon have to come to terms with the dialect and accents. Of course I could understand Brian but John and Mary were hard to catch and understand all the time. "Ah, sure, there's no fear of them," she said when I asked how the dogs were. I soon interpreted this as they were OK. Then Brian joined in, enjoying speaking to Irish folk in their own back yard again.

"Terry's not a bad lad but he's not much cop on." To which they all laughed loudly. He was telling the truth really, telling them that I wouldn't be a problem but I'm not the sharpest, certainly in terms of practical things. He was referring to the fact that I arrived there without being able to drive, I think, which was a surprise to them as much as my madness in arriving with two retired greyhounds. Yet this first meeting with the Crottys in their home, mirrored that first day in Ireland with Larry. Hospitality is a word which can be exaggerated for the sake of politeness but their welcome was as warm and genuine as anyone could hope for.

The next morning, after a steady night in the Old Mill, Brian prepared to leave for Roscommon. He wished me well and I thanked him more than his grumpy Yorkshire heart might appreciate. I'd always liked Brian and his steadfast, uncomplicated ways and I owed him much. It was he who sold me Daisy and encouraged me to visit Larry's kennels in the first place and, furthermore, without his efforts, I may not have washed up in O'Brien's Bridge. As he drove off from Kate's in his old, familiar, green saloon dog carrier, I sensed the reality of the day. From here on in I was on my own. Or so I thought.

The next day I walked over the Bridge to John and Mary's to take Daisy and Ollie for their morning walk. It was dark and early as I tried to prepare them for the coming week's routine. They'd slept in a draughty, healthy kennel which was guaranteed to provide plenty of fresh Irish air. When I sneaked around to them I could hear them stir and picked up a subtle, unproblematic whinge…the sort which might have been saying, "Where have you been? You bring us all this way and bugger off for a night on the tiles!" Anyway, fast on the lead, we set off for our first morning walk in County Clare, down the canal side, past a number of detached houses, some with smoke already sneaking into the morning air. The only sound was the crunch of footsteps and occasional bouts of sniffing as Ollie and Daisy questioned their new surroundings. We then strolled back on our tracks and walked down the main street in the village. An odd car passed by, while a strolling man said, "How are you?"

"Fine, thank you," I said.

"Lovely morning." Lord, I thought, don't I sound like an Englishman, and I'm not even one of them in the first place! I walked down to the Bridge, struck by the quiet of the early hour. The dogs were having a fresh old time in a new situation with plenty to sniff and a breakfast to look forward to. I sat by the river and talked to them both, whispering, "this is it, girls, told you so. Behave yourselves and I'll do the same and we should be OK." I think they listened pretty well. At least they didn't answer back and they also seemed to miss the startling black cat as it flew past the Old Mill door. Or maybe they had worked out that chasing cats was not on the agenda, certainly if we didn't want to upset the locals!

I tried to establish the start of a routine for Daisy and Ollie, returning them to the Crotty's after the walk, putting them in the kennel and pretending to set off for work. That would be the routine from Thursday onwards, so better get used to it. I locked them in and started to leave the yard as their three pet dogs yapped and alerted John. He lifted his head quickly and rushed to the door. "Where are you going?" That was it, straight into their warm and cosy kitchen, cup of tea and porridge with honey. Mary joined us soon and they outlined their day. Feeding the dogs in the kennels here, then feeding the dogs 'in the bog', then feeding the horses before a run out to trial dogs. It was a new way of life to me but old hat for them. It underlined the difference between their world and my past life, where every day for forty-five years had started with concrete and noise, haste and chase. Thanking them for their hospitality, I went back to the B and B. Kate said she would show me the routine as far as the bus service was concerned as I needed to get into Limerick and open a bank account. No Irish bank account, no pay, I reminded myself.

We waited across the road from Kate's house. A large, high riding white bus arrived, more like a luxury coach. Getting on the bus, Kate introduced me to Podge, saying I'd moved here. We travelled at a married man's pace towards Castleconnell and beyond, picking up locals of all shapes and sizes, all with a friendly word for Podge. He knew everyone and everyone knew Podge. In the background, country music played away as I looked out of the windows, left and right, not having enough time to take stock of the beautiful scenery. It took me back to that night in the Bridge with my old mates, Paul and Chris and my disbelief that people actually lived here. It wasn't a holiday home, it was a home, a community in the most awe inspiring scenery. And as I looked and listened to Podge welcoming 'Orla' and 'Pa', I asked myself, under hidden breath, "Is this real? And am I really here?" It then began to strike me that I would be enjoying such a journey every day into work and every day back home.

As I got off the bus, Podge said, "We'll see you again, Terry." In all my life in Yorkshire, I am certain that no bus driver ever called me by my name, nor was so welcoming. There it was a case of pay your fare, grab a seat and simply bide your time going from one part of the industrial north to another. As I considered this very pleasant culture shock, I made my way around Limerick city centre.

First of all I needed a bank to open an account. No problem. I went to the Bank of Ireland, all my documents in place, bank details from Yorkshire, utility bills, passport, council tax bills and so on. I told the member of staff that I needed an account before going to work on Thursday, so that I could set up my pay arrangements. However, despite having everything I needed to prove who I was in the UK, I had nothing to prove who I was in Ireland! I needed proof of my job and proof of my address. The fact was, I was in a totally different country and my past counted for nothing. For a second or two I started to think I had a lot to do to prove my identity, especially when I also had to go to the Social Welfare Office to prove I was eligible to work in the first place. This introduction to a new bureaucracy was another quick reminder that I was in a foreign country, a new world. I smiled, admiring the differences between the world of my past and this new world. Small things but big differences, I thought. Yet heart-warming.

I then walked to my place of work as much to find out where the office was but also to try and get some proof of identity from the Department of Justice. Walking down O'Connell Street, passing shops and eateries, I started to come across offices and other banks. As I looked to cross the road, I held back sharply like you do when you grasp a stinging nettle. In front of me was a soldier, camouflaged and armed. To his left there were two others, again armed and a further three to my right, plus an armoured vehicle. I was startled. I tried to take the situation into account quickly, work out what was going on, without panicking myself. Then the penny dropped. I worked out that they were providing security for a bank. If not, there were robbers inside who were due to be welcomed to a bloody and prescribed party! I moved on, my first day in Limerick city and another reminder that I was in a different world, different to me at least.

Within minutes I entered Lower Mallow Street Probation Office for the first time. I'd spoken to Ger Quigley previously before coming over and in real life he was as helpful and charming as he was on the phone. Though work was a couple of days away, it was good to meet people and useful to ask for a bit of local advice. There was a real buoyancy about the place, a positive glow that I'd not come across often in the past. People came and went as Ger introduced me, the new lad. I went upstairs and met Margaret, my manager, whose enthusiasm had jumped out of the phone at me when I had previously spoken to her from North Wales. I recalled our first conversation very well. Her use of the word 'bloody' was regular and necessary as it helped accentuate her passion for the job. As I left the office I was certain that I was going to enjoy life there. One thing that struck me again was the pace of some of the talking and the odd, new phrases that had skipped by me when I'd visited the area before, such as, 'not a bother on me', 'Aw, he's a ginnit'. I'd get used to it, I thought. As for the physical environment, there was none of the usual graffitti on a probation wall that you'd find in England. 'Hickey is a pillock' and 'Judge Scott is a tosser' are two notable trademarks from Bradford that flashed back into my memory. As I wandered down the steps to the exit, I wondered if they ever had 'offenders' in the building, given how clean and smart it was. Not a dozing, dazed heroin user in sight, not a drunk banging at the reception window.

The next day was the last before I officially started my career in the Irish Probation Service. I had breakfast with John and Mary, this time a full Irish with a pot of tea. Was I on holiday or was this just another day? I remember thinking that I should make the most of the winter sunshine on my last day of liberty, so I walked Daisy and Ollie for a couple of miles, much of it with hardly a soul in sight. The River Shannon was as inspiring as every other time I had seen it, going from a north easterly direction towards Limerick in the south west. I spent time breaking the walk, sitting and shaking my head at the beautiful scenery, hardly believing that I was here. To live and work. How would it go, how would it develop? How would I fit in, would I understand what life meant to local people and would they understand me? Would working here result in the same lifestyle as before? Just a different scene in different colours with different sounds? Certainly I couldn't predict events but the look from Daisy was a 'don't worry, Dad, we'll be fine'.

My first day at work demanded a very early start, walking and feeding the dogs, then back to Kate's for a shower and shave. On with the suit, briefcase under the arm, packed only with yesterday's Racing Post. The driver said, "How are you?" Again I found myself being polite, just as my mother told me to!

"I'm fine and yourself?" Then, yes, very odd indeed, the children on the bus were well-behaved. I'd never been on a bus like that before. I was used to being on a bus where empty cans of coke would be rolled or even chucked down the aisle, where every four or five words were split with a vulgar expletive, the 'c' or the 'f' word. These kids know how to behave, I thought.

Getting to work was 'D day', my landing for the protracted battle. I hadn't a clue what to expect but I felt I was on the biggest learning curve, as they say, that any middle-aged Welsh lad in Ireland had ventured on. As I wandered down O'Connell Street towards the office, I had a quick word with the Good Lord, reminding him that even though I was a protestant by upbringing and had committed far too many sins without confession, could he please keep me safe? I went into a shop close to the junction with Lower Mallow Street, fell in love, there and then, with the lady making sandwiches and suddenly felt that everything might be OK.

When I got to the office I was as nervous as a virgin teenager…anxious not to be judged too harshly and praying that if I couldn't perform to expectations, my fumbles and mistakes would first be forgiven and then forgotten. Sheesh, I was so nervous. Should I try and control my natural accent as strong as Yorkshire tea, so that people could understand me? Or had they seen Emmerdale or the film 'The Full Monty'? Within minutes I was doing the round of introductions again, everyone so welcoming, most with a derivative of the same question.

"What brings you to Ireland then?" Of course the reply was pretty consistent with my comments during the interview when I was asked why I wanted to come to Ireland and work in the Probation Service. Funny, I thought, both then and many, many times since. When millions of Irish people have travelled the world, I guess many will have gone for work and a fresh start for a challenge, for security. So I have often been surprised when I've been asked as to my own reasons for being in Ireland. By the time I left that very first day, I think I had ended up saying, "it's all because of Daisy."

The next day was much the same. Introductions, reading essential legal documentation and starting to find out more about life in Limerick. Margaret drove me to the Moyross Estate to see an annual presentation of awards to young people. This was a crime prevention initiative supported by many partners, including Probation. Travelling to the Ceim ar Ceim centre, I saw the estate at close face and its expanse reminded me of the Grove, where I grew up in Halifax. As for the presentation it lifted me enormously to see lads who had started to educate and improve themselves amidst the negative demands of their environment. There was a buzz, a sense of real achievement provided by the young people who had gained recognition for a change as opposed to criticism and damnation. There was also a sense of pride and achievement for those staff and volunteers who had given so much. I still remember some of the faces, the characters, including Danny, who would be one of my cases when I later went to work in the prison.

That Friday passed very positively at work and I prepared myself for my first weekend in Ireland as a resident, a 'blow in' as they say. I tried to do some new things, induct myself as much as I could. This included lunch and a few pints in Limerick, an odd bit of shopping and further exploration of the countryside. And, of course, time with Mr and Mrs Crotty, trying to get to grips with their accents, especially John's. I also had some serious work to do, looking for somewhere to stay. Yet my first full week at work soon beckoned and it proved to be a turning point. I went to Court as part of the induction and Margaret took me in to meet Judge Tom O'Donnell, which went well. First impressions were that he was a gentleman, who wanted to work with the Probation Service, wanted to instill and impart justice. As court started I was struck immediately by the number of people in the public gallery. It was packed. In England that would normally only occur in high profile cases, yet here we were, crammed full to the point where there were numbers standing up, pressed against the wall. As for the process, it was pragmatic and effective. I have never seen so much business dealt with in one Court room so quickly, without fuss and without pomp and show. The English Magistrates Court system could learn much from this. Defendants were called and they stood up, there and then. "What happened here then, Inspector?" the Judge would ask the prosecuting Garda. Hardly any pleas of 'not guilty', the four solicitors each processing their business without complicating matters.

The custody cases, i.e., those in custody with the Gardai or in Limerick Prison, again produced something I had not seen before. Two particular defendants came into the dock surrounded by a number of casually posed Garda. As they appeared, a couple of rugged looking youths turned to face them, no words being uttered but their slow and lengthy glare was almost as threatening as a blade to the neck. I saw this the first day I was in Limerick District Court and have seen exactly the same type of intimidation on many occasions when I have been there since then. The feuding and gang-related troubles go right into the court arena, bare faced and brazen. Almost giving a reminder to the public and authorities that they will not be stopped in their quest to intimidate.

So I left court, again having it confirmed that the Irish District court system was very different from the English and Welsh system. It was refreshing, so pragmatic and appeared to be effective. I was impressed. But I was also concerned. Again I had problems understanding the language clearly. When some protagonists in proceedings spoke, it was hard to pick up every word. In fact I don't think if I am being totally honest that I understood half! Yet my general experience of court helped get me by. It wasn't my hearing I'm sure, but rather the pace of the language and the occasional broken sentences which were part and parcel of local communication. Still, as they say, I got the giste. The rest of the week included further induction and more time getting familiar with the Irish legal system. So, it was with relief that I picked up my first few cases. Wherever you go, the legal system may be different, the processes may vary and justice might be evident or not. Nevertheless, one thing is for sure. Human behaviour is human behaviour, though local culture plays a significant role.

I remember those early cases well. Cahill was the first. A slim, athletic man used to violence received and violence dished out. A rich mop of tar black hair. A roguish smile on a good day, a cut-throat glare on any other day. He had a smile that could open a tin of salmon. Some of Limerick's very worst tried to kill him one day. They failed miserably and justice took its course on another day. They always do a bloody good funeral in Limerick, whoever the corpse. Yet it was a Probation Order for Assault for now and he indicated as much as he cared to that he wasn't averse to giving friends, relatives and enemies a good kicking, if justice required.

Then there was Joe, out on bail and subject to what they term 'adjourned supervision'. How he was not remanded in custody, I don't know. He got drunk with his best friend as you do. He then tried to carve him up with a knife as you do. He regretted the offence, not because of the impact on the victim but because of the consequences on himself and his family. Then there was Wayne. Lovely lad, butter wouldn't melt in his mouth. Again, he'd got totally drunk, saw his mate look fondly at his girlfriend then decided to puncture a hole in his back. These were the first few cases on my books, all with common themes, violence, often to the edge of a fatality, always drink related. Yet they were out in the community. And of course there was John, a face as innocent as a cherub choir boy but with a record of aggression which told a different story.

Yes, it was a good week all round. I left work that night thinking I'd come all this way to Ireland for a new life but I needed something very familiar, a Friday night treat. Before setting off back to Kate's for my second weekend in O'Brien's Bridge, I found my way into Dunne's stores on Henry Street, Limerick. Eyes peeled, I just bought the bare essentials as I'd planned to eat in the Old Mill for much of the weekend. So, yes, the bare essentials, a couple of bottles of Chilean red, strong cheese, ham and crusty bread. Oh, yes, plus one of those king size bars of Cadbury's Dairy Milk. You know the ones. Anyway, twelve hours after getting home from Limerick, I was up bright and early, hangover in action, just ready to be blown away by an early morning walk. It was like being on holiday. Here I was in the only place I wanted to be with the only people I wanted to be with, Daisy and Ollie. It couldn't be much better, I thought.

We walked from the Bridge in the direction of Castleconnell. I can still remember shaking my head every now and again. Is this really my lovely weekend off or am I still on holiday? The dogs felt the same, I swear they did. A sense of being in a new place was a good thing for them. Surely they could swallow the clear air as readily as myself, sensing the difference from urban British life? They certainly sensed the movement of swans and ducks and birds who were obviously in the area for the same reason as myself. Because they wanted to be here. Walking back towards the village, we settled at a breakfast table by the river side. John's brother Christy waved over as he peered out of his doorway which looked directly onto the river. "Dirty old day," he said, which I assumed referred to the weather. But, as always, the Irish weather never bothered me. 'Dirty old days' only hit home when you are in urban chaos, rushing and pushing, forever responding to your watch. We walked up the street. I leaned into the Butcher's, Daisy and Ollie sniffing with a vengeance. I bought half-a-dozen large eggs for the dog's breakfast over the weekend and Ray the Butcher threw in a couple of bones. It was a lovely start to the day and I was grateful and pleased. Yet sometime next week I would have to pursue my longer term accommodation needs and with the dogs to look after, I sensed that I might have no other choice but to look well away from the Bridge. Still, as I wandered up to John and Mary's, I reminded myself that I couldn't have everything. Just to be alive in this beautiful country, starting a new life was more than I could ask for.

After feeding the dogs and putting them in the paddock, I heard the tap on the window to come inside for some tea. As Mary brewed up, John fried up. We talked about my week and how I was settling in at work, and where to buy this and that. I loved their company from the off. And, while a few words might have passed me by, I was keen to learn the local language, the phrases which many, many times brought a smile and often a laugh. They told me of their time in England, John as a builder and Mary as a clippie on the buses. They talked of the times when their journey away from their home was typical of many young Irish people. In their day, unemployment meant there were few options if any at all. We would talk a thousand times more in the coming years as I tried to understand life in an Irish rural community. But for today, talk turned back to the practicalities.

They assured me that the dogs could stay with them until I had sorted suitable accommodation, which was a big help. I had already looked through papers and on the internet and knew that rental options with dogs were limited and I certainly couldn't buy anything with my Yorkshire home nowhere near being sold. I said I had the chance to look at a house in Killaloe, a pretty area eight kilometres or so away. At this point John said they had a house they were building, a mile outside the village which needed looking after. Mary had thought it would be too big for me and more importantly, too far off the beaten track, compared to what I was used to. No, no, I insisted, I'd like to take a look.

The next morning John and I set off in his steely red charger, the van that carried anything. People, shopping, livestock and dead stock. Leaving the village over the narrow canal bridge, there was a sign post saying 'Killaloe 8km' and a metre away, another sign post saying 'Killaloe 9km'. What did it matter, what was a kilometre between friends, especially when they both pointed in the right direction? We travelled down the long straight road, fields of horses to the roadside backing onto acres of bogland in the distance before rising up to fields in a dozen shades of green. On the right side of the road, a few hardy sheep wandered up the canal bank in the bright sunshine, making the most of the clement winter weather. As the van passed five houses on the left in a half-mile stretch, we turned the bend where a long road went into the distance. Three hundred metres down the road we pulled up at what I considered a farmer's gate. The last house we passed to get there was well over a one hundred and fifty metres away and the only house in sight of the farmer's gate was a further forty metres down the Killaloe Road. The next house down the road towards Killaloe was not in sight as the road stretched mile by mile between a friendly canopy of trees.

Getting out of the van, I immediately saw the house about forty metres from the road, up a path of stone and slate chippings leading to the dark brown front door. To the side of the house was a vast undulating field, at least eight acres in size, bordered on one side by a river and in the distance, some two hundred metres away by trees and fencing. Beyond the trees I could see large cattle on adjacent farmland but not a house in sight on the level. The backdrop to this stunning scene was the extension to the Clare Hills, rising hundreds of feet up in the distance. I could spot no more than a couple of houses many miles away as the scenery drifted into a picture which prompted only one image to my eye – Heaven.

When we went inside he told me that they had considered moving up there at some stage but never felt the drive to leave O'Brien's Bridge as yet. The market had fallen out in terms of selling and it remained as John put it 'a project', which he was having no urge to complete in haste. They had no plans at this time and as I walked around the solid house created by John, I considered the ridiculous and impossible prospect of staying there for however long. The house was large with four bedrooms. The kitchen, sitting and living rooms, all felt right. For a boy who had spent most of his life in tight urban council housing estates, this was open space in a rural paradise.

As we looked out of the window towards the expanse of the Clare Hills, John asked if I was interested in looking after the property until I got settled in the area. Rent, in terms of cash, was never an issue for him as he was solely concerned about ensuring that the unfinished house was heated and safe from vandalism, especially given that nearby was a residential care home for difficult juveniles. So, we made a gentleman's agreement. I would look after the house as he continued his 'project' and as soon as either of us wanted to change the situation we would happily make other arrangements. While all I needed was a roof with a view, all John needed was a live in security guard, someone who he could trust. Someone to look after the house as it grew, keeping it warm while looking after the animals. I could not believe my good fortune. Maybe God was a Welshman after all.

As we left for the van, John introduced me to the two horses, Sinbad, Rummy and then Fred the donkey as he fed them their breakfast. Looking back to those creatures on that day, I was just another passing visitor. To me, their presence in that beautiful field in that idyllic setting would be a permanent picture of a new way of life.

# 6 – Life in Knockadrehid: The Early Days

On giving Kate notice that I would be leaving in a couple of days, she very kindly gave me some bedding and bits of crockery, again testament to her generosity and warmth. She was a lovely, quiet lady but I could sense that she had been a devil in her day. A few days later I thanked her for giving me a start to my life in Ireland, then made my way to Knockadrehid for my first evening outside the village. As I settled the dogs for the night, I had my first sense of what life would become.

I reclined for the evening in the large kitchen, listening to local radio stations, Limerick and Clare. The dogs lay on a carpet by my feet as I cupped milky coffee and treated myself to custard creams. Listening to the radio was something that I had forgotten to do, having spent many years focused on the TV. For the first few weeks before I bought a TV, it was refreshing to hear local dialect and local news. There was, once again, the reminder that this was a different world. Reports of local events, of court hearings, obituaries, traffic problems across the county and, of course, the GAA. That passion I first encountered on the train from Dublin to Limerick on my first trip was recited many times. It made me ask the questions, in the years to come, why the GAA was so important being so uniquely Irish? I learnt pretty quickly that it was more than sport.

And, of course, there was the music. The music which again had a traditional stamp all over it, which, in itself made me think of Wales. If there was one thing, beyond Rugby, that the Welsh rely on to distinguish their character, it is their music. While I listened in those early days to either silence or the radio, Irish music and tales of legendary artists always concluded the evening. When the music stopped and the lights stood dark and still, I gathered my thoughts and thanked God for my place in life. For the rest of that first week in Knockadrehid, John and Mary would call up with one thing or another to help me be more comfortable. They were helpful and considerate from day one and yet they soon appreciated how much I loved my space in their rambling old house. On Friday evening I christened my first weekend there with a bottle of red, while Daisy and Ollie were treated to celebratory bones.

That first weekend was memorable. On Saturday, after the customary coffee with John and Mary, I asked if they knew of an enjoyable walk without travelling into the village. John suggested that I turn left out of the gate and head along the Killaloe Road, turn left at the first junction and then keep turning left down the country road. It would, he said, "Keep you busy for a mile or so and bring you back to the house in a circle." As simple as that. And so I set off, enjoying the peace of the road, crossing the river as it left the field, viewing miles of greenery littered with inquisitive red and white bulls. As we walked towards Killaloe, I talked to the dogs, introducing them to the locality. Occasionally, a car would come towards us and then veer to the middle of the road, so as to give us time to walk safely. When this first happened I could not understand why. Maybe I shouldn't have been on the road in the first place. Yet, as it happened, time and time again and as I acknowledged each considerate manoeuvre with a smile and a wave, I sensed this was normal driving practice in the country...something I can never recall happening in West Yorkshire, even on the few quiet roads. You'd always be squeezed up against a wall as a car came towards you. It was as if there were different rules here, perhaps a polite driver's code based on a greater understanding of animals and country life.

So, we went on, talking as we went...left off the main road and left and left and so on. And, yes, John said it would be a grand walk. We arrived back some three-and-a-half hours later, during which time I learnt something about the Irish language. Never take time or distance literally! It was a long introduction to the locality, a stunningly beautiful one at that. When we got through the gate, I let the dogs off as they saw the field stretched in front of them. Yet they could only manage as far as their bowl of water and after their dinner, I heard nothing of them for the next eighteen hours! The next morning John called up and asked how the walk went, a glint in his eye devilishly exposing the fact that he set me up. "Lovely, John, yes, it was a grand walk as you said." And it had been. That wouldn't be the last time that John Crotty would set me up.

The following week I was in to the routine of leaving the house at a quarter to eight and waving down the bus on the main road, which was another new experience. The driver, Tom, was standing in for the legendary Seamus, who was off ill. I soon found out why Seamus was of such renowned fame. He was a punctual driver, very punctual in fact. He was always bang on time providing you worked out that you needed to be at the pick-up point at least five minutes early. And what a driver. I will swear that he never broke the speed limit but he always got you there before time, providing there was no hazard on the way. He was the most reliable man behind a wheel that I can remember, though you could say the same about Jimmy and Podge. Not only do they serve a pick-up-and-drive function but they flavour the day with their personality and provide a genuine warmth on a cold winter's day.

Getting to know these Bus Eireann drivers was getting to know Ireland itself. Nothing less than enjoyable. Having travelled in unreliable modes of public transport in the UK, I began to realise that Irish Bus and Rail travel were far more reliable and comfortable. The fact that these local drivers take time to talk and have the craic is a great bonus. Seamus, Jimmy and Podge seemed to know everywhere, everybody and almost everything. Seamus would always greet you with the weather and 'how are you'. Jimmy would often greet you with 'How's year day been, Terry'? Or 'Nothing strange'? Podge, well, Podge was the perpetually jovial driver, who occasionally popped out the 'f' word but only in the right company. Whenever you met Podge's bus as you walked along the pavement, he'd peep his horn and cross himself as though he'd seen the Pope. Likewise Jimmy, who would say hello with the horn and beam that lovely warm smile of his.

If only the bus company paid these drivers their true weight in gold for their customer service, they'd be millionaires. They have the civility and thought to look after vulnerable and less mobile passengers and were disciplined enough to make sure that any child travelling on their bus behaved themselves. It did not take me long to realise that Irish schoolchildren travelling on these buses were far, far better behaved than any group of their peers in urban West Yorkshire. This, again, is one of the beauties of rural life in Ireland. I have no doubt, whatsoever, that despite the rigours of the teaching of the Catholic faith, there are very few angels jumping on Bus Eireann with their schoolbags. Nevertheless, I am certain that the very, very vast majority know how to behave and show respect to other passengers. Why? I'm not sure but I still think certain things like good manners are taught as attributes, not weaknesses. Also, of course, I'd be equally certain that Podge, Seamus and Jimmy would know their parents and any unacceptable behaviour could easily be exposed to family discipline!

The following weekend John and Mary called up for coffee and a chat. They also came to collect my rubbish, thus saving me a fortune. John also did two things that day which I'll not forget easily. The first was to ask my help in securing the horses and Fred the donkey within the electric fence. He no doubt remembered Brian Gillard's comment that I had 'no cop on' as he asked me to pick up the wire from the ground. Being keen to get used to rural life, I did so readily, grabbing the wire without a second thought. As I did so, I immediately felt a heavy bolt of electric and my reflexes did the rest. Spontaneously, John laughed out in the wicked knowledge that he had, for want of a phrase, got me. Mary briefly pulled him up for his devilment but only briefly as she saw the funny side of it all. Myself too. I was beginning to settle in and had already learnt that I needed to learn quickly if I was to survive…and I had to watch Mr Crotty! The second thing John did that day was to give me Christy Storan's phone number.

# 7 – Christy Storan

For a non-driver and for those many late night drunks needing to be taken home from Darby's or Bonner's, Christy was vital. He was described as 'not a taxi driver – but he'd take you anywhere for a few euros'. When I first rang him in December 2008, he was already aware that I'd be calling for a job or two. Mary had told him that I was new to the area and besides needing transport, I would need pointing in the right direction. Christy was the man. He was a former colleague of Seamus, Podge and Jimmy, having worked for many years as a driver with Bus Eireann. Rumour has it that he retired for health reasons. One story was that he developed health complications through diabetes and became seriously ill with cancer. He is said to have been close to death many times and there is even one tale about him having died, at least twice. There is the other story, the more accepted version, of course. This is the one where Christy slipped on a banana skin as he was getting off the bus. No one knows where the banana skin came from but it led to his professional downfall. He was unfit to drive and while he was offered 'office duties', he declined. He was paid off with a lump sum and a regular monthly payment from Zurich Insurance. This was Christy Storan, ex-trainee butcher, ill-fated bus driver and friend to all.

I met Christy for the first time when I called for a lift to go shopping. He was lightweight build, possibly 5ft 8in but he was full of beans and energy from the off. It didn't take me long to realise that Christy was good fun and great company. Some people said he was a form of taxi driver for locals but he was never that. I never knew taxi drivers who could tell a tale like Christy, deliver laundry or food or even bring glasses around when there were extra guests at the dinner table. Nor can I recall any taxi driver who had such a rich and very clearcut outlook on life. He wouldn't have made a politician, our Christy, as he was often too ready to call a spade a spade, regardless of the situation. Though, when I think of it, he often expressed many opinions which would have made him popular if standing as a prospective TD!

For example, Christy on crime and punishment was a revelation. He'd often repeat that "they should send them to Cuba, that would put manners on them. Give 'em the cat o' nine tails, they need a good beating."

"I'll do it myself for nothing." He'd add that "prison is too good for them; hang 'em, they're nothing but scum". Christy also had a specific answer to the local feud.

"It's easily done, Ter, they know who they are, just take 'em out, that's all they need to do, take one or two out." Yet Christy was a soft soul for anyone he knew who was in trouble with the law, including a young lad convicted of drug dealing.

"He's a lovely, lad, Ter, from a lovely family in the city. His parents are good people…they don't know what went wrong." Forgetting the fact that his offending bolstered up the drug trade and thus created many victims of crime, Christy's heart of gold would take over.

"He was a lovely boy, never done wrong and prisons not for lads like him. Can you do something for him, Ter?" Of course I never could and Christy understood that.

Christy on other locals was an entertainment in itself and he'd pride himself on his 'confidentiality'. And you'd always want to believe him. Yet on one occasion he dropped a female friend of mine off in nearby Killaloe. A few days later, John probed me over the young lady in Killaloe! So much for confidentiality! I learnt then that any romantic arrangements, even with single women, could come at a price. Speak to a single woman at a bus stop and you might as well be sleeping with her. Speak to a married woman at a bus stop and the husband would soon be turning up at your door with a meat cleaver. Not that Christy fostered that sort of scandal. It was village life, full stop. Yet his comments about his other 'clients' as he called them, tickled me. There was the bonny young woman who drove him mad... "Don't call me your 'love', I'm not your 'love'." She'd ring and he would refuse to answer in fear of her calling him 'love' time and time again. Then there was Tully, Pat and old Cussack, plus countless other lads who Christy safely ferried home after a night of drunken revelry in Bonners and Darbys. Christy provided a public service at a cheap rate but, as I said, he was never a 'taxi', just a friend who gave lifts and received friendship and some petrol money in return. And he was a gambler and a tipster. A legend of one at that.

He'd often pop into the bookies in Killaloe or Castleconnell and wait for me while I did my shopping. I'd meet him in the bookies for half an hour's punting before I set off home with 'the messages', a term for the shopping. The staff knew him well, as did every punter in any betting shop in the area. "Have you anything today, Christ?"

"I have, I fancy Darcy's mount in the novice chase," he said as we mingled with a dozen or so in the shop in Castleconnell.

"I've heard he'll make all the running and leave them standing." Of course that led to a flurry of bets, tenners, twenties, fifty each way and so on. I couldn't resist twenty euros each way myself at sixteen to one and then nipped outside to text Chris and Paul back in England. Back into the shop, the crowds gathered around the screens and Darcy's horse, Orpheus Valley, made the running as predicted. However, the screen blinked and faulted every ten or fifteen seconds, breaking off the coverage every now and again. Each time the race came back into sight, the tip was still leading as, one by one, his rivals tried to land a telling challenge.

As the race approached the three mile mark, two furlongs out, each and every eye watched the screen in anticipation for the horse to fall or blow up and fade out of the running. Again, the picture broke up to a chorus of 'feck, feck' only to return to see Christy's sixteen to one shot cross the line fifty yards clear! I picked up my four hundred and forty euros, gave Christy a hug and said, "You're a feckin genius." He received the applause of everyone who backed the horse as each and everyone shook their heads in disbelief. The horse had trotted up. My mates, Paul and Chris, rang to thank him, chuffed to pieces that he was happy enough to share his information with two Englishmen. That was Christy. A friend of yours would always be treated like a friend of his. A generous soul to say the least. And, of course, he had 'friends in high places'.

He would get information from Duggan and other local racehorse owners, plus contacts that he made as an owner in the past. Much of the information was linked to organised betting coups, some in Ireland and some in England. It always seemed to be good information because I can never recall one of his tips not being heavily backed. One such gamble revolved around a horse called 'The Winged Assassin'. Chris had been over, had met Christy and thanked him for his sixteen to one winner. Christy had hoped to get some information for Chris while he was over but by the time Christy dropped Chris off at the train station, there'd been no tip in those two days. However, within minutes of the train setting off, Christy received a call to back The Winged Assassin as it 'was expected' in England. We made for the nearest betting shop, William Hills, not far from the Locke Bar. I texted Chris and he asked me to put a tenner each way on for him for fun. Christy entered the shop and put two-hundred euros on the nose as I backed it each way for Chris and myself. It started at nine to two and bolted in with an amazing turn of foot, just as you'd hope for a horse laid out to win. Christy gave that Christy smile, no cockiness, just a knowing look as we picked up our winnings. He went to buy extra mince for his twenty or so cats and I bought a chicken for Daisy and Ollie. Yes, he had good contacts and friends in high places. His 'contacts' with Dermot Weld provided many a winner, especially at Galway. In fact, I'm writing this now on my laptop, affectionately called Dermot, bought out of my Christy-inspired winnings at the 2010 Galway Festival. Yet his friends in high places reached even further beyond that legendary Irish trainer.

One Saturday morning, I recall him ringing me to say he anticipated a 5/1 winner that afternoon and the best price was in the bookmakers in Killaloe. I needed to shop so we set off, after, of course, taking Christy's instructions to let Paul and Chris know. We got in the bookies, ten minutes before the off and Christy had his standard two hundred on, myself, a modest, but hopeful twenty at 4/1. Yet again, Christy delivered the goods and again, he went next door to Supavalue to buy a treat for his cats. Likewise, I did the same for Daisy and Ollie, plus a couple of bottles of Argentinian Red. As he drove me back to Knockadrehid on his way to pick up Tully from Bonners, we both bathed in the good mood that a nice winner brings you and a winner from Ireland's greatest tipster at that. Soon the phone rang. "Hello," he started in his usual 'pick up a taxi fare voice', only to hear the local priest on the phone. He was exultant, euphoric and grateful for the tip from Christy and delighted that he got the early price of five to one! I chuckled quietly and discreetly as Christy said, "I'm pleased, Father, I'm pleased so and it won well!" I could hear the Good Father on the line and I would swear he had started celebrating even before I opened my own first bottle!

Of course there were occasional losers but Christy had an excellent strike rate, all at reasonable prices. If he had stuck to backing his own tips he'd have done very well for himself. Yet his popularity wasn't just because of his tips. He was a much called for all-rounder. Often he'd be asked to sing a song or two in the local pubs as he waited for a bevy of drunks to finish one last pint or so. He was also known as a water diviner and by all accounts he had a good strike rate, including divining the well for my nearest neighbour, Don. And, of course, it was perhaps inevitable that he had a brief run as a bookmaker at the Markets Field dog track, ploughing in much of his compensation from the banana skin accident. Unfortunately, that venture didn't last long. Rumour has it that on one evening, the row of established bookies took exception to the new face on the block. One by one they laid off bets at ruinous prices on Christy and the outcome was inevitable. But he bounced back as always, somehow bringing a smile and an endearing phrase to light up the day.

In those early years Christy not only provided an unorthodox taxi role, providing tips, delivering all sorts of goods but he introduced me to local people and essential facilities. These included Pat Stapleton and his wife Bridget. If you ever need a smart, short old-fashioned haircut, go to Pat's Barbershop on O'Connell Street in Limerick. Pat was a champion bike rider in the '60s but he learnt his trade as a barber in 1945, since when he has cut the hair and shaved the chins of many a man. In his early eighties now, he still does the business with the eye of an eagle and the steadfast hand of a heart surgeon. He had a stroke some years ago and has difficulty in speaking. Yet he opens up six days a week at 7.30 a.m, Bridget alongside him, and still works and entertains. The inside walls of his shop are covered in pictures, poems and comments on life that would inspire or humour anyone. Every time you sit in that barber's chair you feel that wee bit special. Not only do you get a bloody good haircut but you wave your eyes around the room, taking in the Pat Stapleton wall show. You feel very, very welcome as you always do in Limerick. But you also feel a bit more grounded, knowing that the man who very carefully cuts your hair does it for the love of the job and despite his health. Different generation and different class, that is Pat and Bridget. As are Niamh and

Seamus, who own Limerick's superb eatery, Brunch. It was Christy who suggested this place on the recommendation of one of his sober 'clients'.

Yes, Christy will forever be a legendary part of O'Brien's Bridge history and, no doubt, throughout other wider communities where he travelled and entertained so many with his words of wisdom and humour. Senior local Gardai, government officers, journalists, drunken mechanics and Welsh probation officers and many others, all experienced many a journey with Christy and shared in his philosophy of life. Even if you didn't agree with his view of things, you'd welcome the hearing of it. He was, as they say, a throwback to a distant era. His values were traditional, his sense of humour endearing and never meant to hurt. Christy was, and is, the entertainer and one of the most generous souls. He once said that he knew what his wake would be like, quiet and low key. I doubt that. Only when he became seriously ill in early 2011, did he start to believe that he had friends.

In fact, only when he became terminally ill did he start to realise that he was not only valued by the community but also loved. Seeing his lively and warm spirit being tested to the limit and watching his unique independence being eroded, was very difficult for those who cared for him, not least his own family, Mary Duggan and his friend Luke. Yet how difficult it was for the man himself; we will never know. A man who generously cared for others, whilst hiding his own emotions and fears, he was often a misunderstood man, at times an unconventional man. He enjoyed his privacy, his animals and, at times, his solitude. Thankfully, however, as Christy faced his demise, he began to realise that people really cared about him, and that he was no longer considered as just the eccentric character who lived alone with a hundred cats in Birdhill.

With no wife, partner, or children, there was always the sense that he was emotionally lonely, primarily choosing to give rather than take, unlike most of us do. One thing is for certain. Christy Storan was both a wise man and an innocent man, and he proved that such qualities can live in harmony while the rest of us can barely live with one of them.

# 8 – Crotty's Field

That first year in Knockadrehid was the time when I discovered contentment and learnt how to keep it. In the first few weeks I felt that I was on an adventure, a voyage of discovery. Being winter I had no early evening light after work but I got used to being outside with the dogs in lamplight as they found their bearings with the horses and old Fred. I managed in the early weeks without a TV and enjoyed that enormously as it gave me time to read and listen to the radio. Every workday I left the office in Lower Mallow Street and by the time I was home, courtesy of the lightning fast Seamus, I was already relaxed. I soon started to get a balance between work and play. On Friday night I either had a pint or two in Limerick before coming home or, on occasions, a pint in the Old Mill in the village. Either way the dogs were OK as John or Mary would always let them out of the garage or feed them if required. Saturday mornings were special as usual. I'd be up early and around the field before John and Mary came around for chat, usually after ten once they'd fed all the other dogs. Over the weekends I got into the healthy routine of feeding the animals, taking long walks down the Killaloe Road or into the village. I'd often sit for hours, winter weather or not, in the rocking chair, perched by the front step or the step facing the hills. From the front I could watch Daisy and Ollie roam at their leisure, up to the front gate while I drank tea and read the paper. The air then was as fresh as it is now and only a very wet day would deny me my weekend time in the rocker.

Yes and it was from that view to the front of the house that I spotted 'The Daffodil'. It was my first spring and as I glanced to a mound of earth facing the door, some ten yards away, my eyes fell on my first daffodil. It was an immediate and warm reminder of Wales and more significantly, Mum. She always loved the Welsh flower, mainly because it symbolised a fresh year, a new beginning. It looked directly on to the front door. Almost looking out at me or looking for me. Though I walked every blade of grass covering the field, I never saw another daffodil that year. I sensed that this was a message sent to reassure me, to make me feel that I would never be alone. Since that first spring and that lone, special daffodil, I have been certain that Mum has come to Ireland with me. I took the flower and pressed it in the Bible. It remains there as an on-going reminder of Mum and the fact that I will never be alone.

Crotty's field is just that, a heartland of peace and tranquillity, though always alive and changing by the seasons. When the heavy rains come as gifts from the Gods, the river changes colour from transparent clear fresh water to a browny-red mix of minerals and mud. Bringing seeds of the mountain with it, the river lifts and turns faster than normal, fish hiding within the darker colours, almost knowing that downstream waits the Fisherman. More rainfall means more water and more sound as the river takes centre stage for the ears and the soul. Sitting on John Crotty's stone in the far corner of the field as the drenching continues, I'm at peace, almost in a dream for as long as I want. Then there are those days when the mist falls into the field, drifting further beyond the trees, providing a warm, comforting blanket. Comforting because you know that when it disappears, the stunning hills will always be there, unlike people and promises. You can count on life in the field.

Around the back of the house I have the view of heaven and the many relaxing and entertaining sounds of nature provided by the birds. In the early months Harry arrived and became a welcomed friend. He was an enormous grey heron, proud as punch if his gait was anything to go by. The first time I saw Harry I watched in awe as he landed down the field in a hollow filled with water. He was motionless for minutes, almost blending in alongside the fence poles. The length of neck and beak was magnificent, popping into the water, no doubt to pull some poor creature out for his dinner. By the time he decided to fly off, mainly in the direction of the Shannon, I had seen well over half an hour of entertainment and a reminder of God's creation. The power and span of the wings spelt independence and freedom. Harry became a legend of the field for many months on his own but more recently in company with one or two others.

When Harry captured my imagination it was very much like the raw magic witnessed by the Boy Casper in the film Kes. Seeing such a beautiful creature stops the clock. And there were so many more creatures in the field which I watched and welcomed and still do. Freddy, the resident fox, for example, is a handsome fella as red as a fox should be, with a brush as big and spectacular as one must be. I have a vivid picture, rock-steady in my mind of the first time I saw the fox. I was out at the side of the house, looking towards the river. Suddenly I caught a glimpse of him crossing the field. Daisy and Ollie seemed to miss him from their relatively low level of sight and I ushered them inside the house. I came out again to see Freddie march in quick-step, covering another thirty yards or so. Then, almost in response to my fiercely focusing eyes, he stopped still like a statue. Motionless for a minute or so, he then came to life again, turning his nose towards me, ensuring that he could see me full on. He didn't gallop off in fear. He simply looked eye to eye with his feet planted firmly in his land, not mine. I didn't move either. I just gazed in admiration until he sped off into the cover, having proved his point. I just wanted him to feel welcome. He came back at night time in the coming weeks. I could hear him in the dark and see his red eyes amidst the desert of the dark in the field. Like every animal that ventured into the field, he was at home as it should be.

In adjacent fields, cattle showed themselves as magnificent specimens. Compared to Kenyan buffalo, the cows and bulls are enormous and if this were safari country, these colourful lumps of brawn and meat would be eulogised. Only the river and the electric fence separates the cattle from ambling greyhounds as they play in opposite fields. For a moment it is reassuring to know that while the life of cattle is relatively short, it is a heavenly one in Knockadrehid. Likewise for the sheep as they nibble on the banks of the canal, trusting their ability to scale slopes which drop steeply into the water. And the lambs, of course, pull a special heartstring, especially for those young at heart. Seeing how these animals live their life before the slaughter is, somehow, reassuring. Knowing that those who make profits from them also provide a sweet life, in a beautiful setting, however, relatively short that is. That is how it should be, what we owe nature, the Creator and each creature.

Then there was the mink. I had never seen a mink before. He came up to the field from the bank of the river. It moved with the grace of a small black panther, almost rolling forward, matching the undulations in the field. It took me some time to work it out. Its blackness was as solid as Welsh coal, its movement as graceful as the Welsh Harp. Fortunately Daisy and then Ollie saw it too late as it made good its escape to the roadside. I prayed that it hadn't run into a car in an effort to escape. Some weeks later I saw the same military like route being followed by the same beautiful cat and smiled knowing that it had survived the first encounter. Yet some animals were destined to show themselves in the field but not survive.

One such creature was an unfortunate rat, early into my first year. Daisy was out for her evening stroll, the darkness clearly restricting her options. Ollie was somewhere around and as usual was the first of the pair to empty out and come back inside. Daisy stayed out longer than usual. Clearly something was bothering her. As the light from the house covered the top part of the drive way, I saw a brief, flashing movement at ground level but not as clearly as Daisy did. From twenty yards to my left she appeared in hunt of the prey and within seconds a high pitched squeal shattered the evening stillness. My first thoughts were of Daisy injuring herself in a chase, given that greyhounds never think of the consequences of their actions beforehand or afterwards for that matter. By the time I caught up with Daisy I saw her blooded nose and felt the intense beating of her powerful tail. I put two and two together and assumed that she'd gone for a cat or the mink and come off second best…but when I washed her nose I noticed that there was no more bleeding. Very odd, I thought.

The next day John came around and as I accounted the tale of last night's events, he knew straight away that she must have killed something quickly, possibly a rat and tore into the stomach. Hence the blood and the very waggy tale. We looked around the front of the house in the bright blue winter light and, sure enough, there lay a dead rat, its stomach ripped by Daisy's shark-like teeth. He said I should move it because it had been known for rat heads to cause infection or poison. This was just another learning experience for the boy from the city as I came to grips with the challenges of my new environment. And there were so many. That field has given me the view to last many a lifetime and taught so many lessons.

And, of course, life with the horses, ponies and Fred the donkey has been another eye opener. Before I moved to Knockadrehid, my experience of horses and the like was limited. The field is so vast that any four-legged beast would have a great playground to enjoy retirement. As for me, I have a video camera in my mind of each and every one of these beauties running, all at different paces but all with the same intention to have fun. Rummy was the biggest of the original three, named by myself after Red Rum, even though she is a lady. It was from Rummy that I learnt the Irish meaning of 'bold'. She wouldn't be adverse to taking a nibble out of man or beast. Then Sinbad, a smaller horse, stout and handsome, white as a medieval charger but without the knight. Then there was Fred. Lord, I loved them all but I really loved Fred. John said he was probably 50 years old and his brother, Christy, who owned Fred, said he was at least that. Maybe that is why Fred and I got on so well. I always made sure that despite Rummy's bold antics, Fred and Sinbad got their share of food and affection. Soon my confidence developed and I would walk amongst them and seek a kiss on the hand. Fred was the shyest, the one who was uncertain. But we soon got on well…nothing that a bag of carrots from the supermarket wouldn't cure. Those three became part and parcel of my very contented life as I spent more and more of my time watching them, talking to them and walking with them.

Those simple activities added to my contentment. But on the day 'The Horseman' came, life in the field was far more vigorous and eye opening than usual. John had agreed to let a couple of horses stay in the field as they needed a few months good feed. In return, The Horseman replaced the shoes on Rummy and Sinbad and agreed to take away a wayward young pony who had been bullying old Fred. It was the sort of trade between horsemen and landowners that goes on regularly, often with no money exchanging hands. The hardest part of the transaction, no doubt, was the removal of the bold and aggressive pony. I looked on inquisitively as John and the Horseman entered the field, trying to separate the horses, aiming to isolate the pony before taking him away to be schooled. Around and around the field the horses went, having great fun, galloping each and every acre. They were having a wonderful time as John and The Horseman, assisted by his young daughter, tracked and hunted down their prey. But the horses, all played the same mischievous game. It went on for twenty minutes, half-an-hour and so on, as sweat beads pumped from the hunters' brows. I wanted to help but was short of ideas other than to think of my own weakness – food.

I pulled half a loaf from the bread bin and walked to a corner of the field whistling sharply and calling out to Rummy.

The old girl recognised the call and as she made her way to the bread, Sinbad ambled along behind for his share. Soon the wayward young pony joined in and within a couple of minutes all three were around me in the corner of the field. While I broke off bread to keep their interest, I waited for the others to arrive. As John cornered the pony down one flank, I kept up the easy part of the snare by dangling pieces of bread. Step by step The Horseman came nearer, knowing he would have but one very brief chance to catch the bold pony. Before I could even guess when he would pounce, The Horseman caught the pony by the neck as it tossed its head violently left and right, ranting defiance in its own rebellious voice. A battle of physical strength and determined wills unfolded for the next few minutes. The Horseman grappled and pulled as the pony shrugged out violently, trying to toss his hunter from his captured neck. The Horseman's feet were briefly taken off the ground by the noble beast but he held on, risking a thump to the jaw and nose. We watched on in awe and respect as The Horseman eventually brought the pony under control, using both strength and compassion. It was the most vivid and unforgettable image of care and control. I had seen nothing like it, either in terms of strength or courage and a will to win from both parties.

Yet in my second winter I learnt the harsh reality of nature once again. First I lost Ollie, sooner than I expected. Within days of going off her food she was diagnosed with liver cancer and there was only one option. I was shattered. We came as three, Ollie, Daisy and myself. It was a heavy loss to lose her. She had been a wonderful racer as Dream of Olwen and an even better friend as Ollie. I'll never forget her beautiful olive eyes and steadfast, honest character. I remember the first night that she came home as a retired greyhound to Yorkshire. She had fits throughout the night, all through anxiety and uncertainty in her new environment. She lay right beside me on the bed, shaking with fear. But like the brave dog she was, Ollie held on to day break and the worst was over. She settled in well with the older bitches, Connie and Flossie, and her personality blossomed over the years. Ollie came with me and Daisy on this life-changing journey. She comforted me and warmed me when I needed it most, just as a true friend does. She now lays in the bog and in my heart. Within days of Ollie going, Daisy took a downfall, going off her food and looking for her best friend. I asked John and Mary if they had a retired dog to home. Enter Casey's Warrior or Casey when he was retired. Within days he was castrated and was sharing his autumn years with pretty old Daisy. I don't think he appreciated losing his landing gear but he settled quickly and well and soon found his place in the Roberts family with the help of the welcoming chicken dinner.

Then there was Fred, the donkey. One morning I looked into the field, as usual, before jumping on the bus. Right at the end of the field I saw Fred lying down. My sharp whistle normally drew the horses and Fred to me in search of a carrot but there was no movement this time. I feared the worst and rang John. He said I should proceed to work as he would be up shortly. We both expected that the worst had happened for this lovely old servant with his turned up toes and wild, white, haircut. I rang John later and it was obvious that Fred hadn't died there and then. Maybe I'd dreamt it, but the good thing was that it made John come up to the house where he did find

Fred after all…in the river. He and his brother Christy hoisted him up with the tractor, chilled and shocked by the flow of the winter water. They made a make-shift stable in the field, warm and cosy. Plenty of straw and hay to eat, plus supplements of carrots and bread. A tarpaulin covered him, stretching over metal poles and he was private and warm and given every chance to get better. We all went down to feed him and turn him as he battled away in the coming days. But as colder weather kicked in, he came to a plateau in terms of his recovery.

Soon the end was inevitable and very compassionate. John rang to say that Christy would call up with someone to put Fred to sleep. I went into the silent, rutted field with hardly a breath coming from my old and cherished friend, Fred. I thanked him as I kissed his noble and weary head. The time was right for him to move on. I went back to the house and stayed inside with the dogs as Christy and a mountain of a man straddled the fence. On his shoulder rested a very long gun. Within a few sobering minutes I heard a shot and thanked Fred for being Fred and God for being God. Throughout that week, from his fall to his death, he had every compassionate and loving chance to recover but never made it. His end was as practical and dignified as his life. It made me think of those people who I had loved and who had died. How they suffered beyond what was necessary. The life and death of Fred reminded me that life is beautiful and life goes on.

Yes, Knockadrehid makes me realise how simple and beautiful life can be. Many times I walk to John Crotty's stone in the far corner of this vast field, sit and listen to the sounds of the nearby river as it runs unchecked at its own pace. I marvel at the wildlife, being entertained and inspired as I discover something different every day. Above, in maturing trees, carved by wind and rain, the birds gather and build nests from where they observe and hunt as they please. They also provide the theme song as greyhounds and horses stretch their vast lungs, galloping freely about the undulating field. They say that "you can't live on fresh air", which is certainly true. However, now I'm convinced that you can't live without it, nor the stone cold, crystal clear water from the house spring. Add a view of heaven, untouched by man's abuse and waste, and Crotty's field has everything. Certainly everything that I would want. If I died tomorrow in this heaven in this beautiful country, I would do so as a very lucky and content man.

Saying all that, I've tried not to think too much as to why I love Knockadrehid. It's a bit like being in love with your soul mate. Some say you should just accept the gift, not question the why and wherefores of your love. Yet my mind wanders on this, probably because I now take less for granted in my life than I ever did. Could it be the raw, natural beauty and a growing admiration for the natural world? Yes, that is part of it, something that every day reminds me that I'm a mere mortal. I'll be gone soon and all this will remain in some shape or form. It's also an appreciation and wonderment of how the birds, fish and animals survive, leading a simple, honest life while we just make things more complex and stressful. The sights, the sounds, the smells and the pace of life. The fun I see, the entertainment I get, the privacy. Yet, when all of this makes sense and when I really don't need to consider the 'whys' for my love, something else comes to mind.

Tonight I walked the field as usual, occasionally lying down then popping up to play ball with Daisy and Casey.

Lazy old things but so relaxing on a warm, blue evening. Then it hit me. As I curved my eyes around and around this beautiful theatre of nature, I sensed a feeling from many years ago. It was though something in my past touched me on the shoulder. I suddenly realised that this field, these surroundings, also made me feel very safe. My mind immediately went back to those long summers that I used to spend at Gran and Grandad's in Trefnant, North Wales. Times when Mum and I escaped the mucky, industrial north and more importantly, when we escaped my Dad for a while. As I played in Crotty's field tonight, just like a young boy free and happy, I recalled those many, many years ago in Trefnant. Then I had the innocence of youth in the field with my football and my imagination, not a soul in sight until Gran, Mum or Amanda called me in for tea. Grandad would look over his brown rimmed glasses at the table as only a village headmaster can, setting me an example for the rest of my life in how to enjoy sport on the television. Gran would smile and feed me in equal portions of love and trust. Mum would be herself again in the house where she grew up and with those who mattered all around her, especially Amanda, who rightly chose to stay with her grandparents rather than suffer my father's behaviour. Those were the only days that I can remember when I really felt happy as a child, those days in Trefnant. Away from Dad, knowing Mum was safe for the while. I loved those days so much that I used to heave in tears when we left. When Gran waved goodbye at the top of the hill until the next time I saw her and Grandad, Amanda and the rest of my family…tonight in Knockadrehid, in Crottys field, that all came back, thank God. And tonight, for all those reasons, I know I deeply love this place. I also know that my heart still has some of that innocence and hope of the young boy in Trefnant.

# 9 – This Sporting Life

Without sport there would probably be no route to a decent life for many of us, including myself. As a child I loved every sport I played, relishing the competition and a chance to prove myself. From my mother's side I suppose I inherited the fair-play, gentleman element in sport. From my father's side I certainly took on his physical attributes as an athlete, though he never pushed me or encouraged me to build on his own achievements as a professional sprinter. Why, I'll never know. Still, I had Mum's passion for all the sports, as she encouraged me to use my time appropriately. And, of course, I was lucky to have a legendary P.E teacher called Mr Bannister. Any developing passion for sport was merely enhanced under Mr Bannister's disciplined leadership. There will be dozens of middle-aged men who could look back at their school days and be thankful for this one teacher's lessons on life at the Highlands School, Halifax. He emphasised the need to always do your best, work as a team and respect the referee's decision. From those early days to now; from athlete, competitor to spectator, these positive influences on my sporting life will always be appreciated. That passion for sport, plus education, surely saved me from a life of crime, while many of my peers drifted into delinquency, trying to make their status through offending. I was lucky…and it was inevitable that my adult life would continue to feed on the healthy feast of sport, not least when I came to Ireland.

Sport marks the calendar as regularly as Easter, Christmas and May Bank Holidays, and as one sporting season ends, another begins. It can lift the spirit, dump the heart to the lowest levels and resurrect our belief in human achievement. It should bring out the best in competitors and supporters, individuals and teams. That is the hope. Pride and glory should be more important than shame and dishonour, regardless of the result. It is not just about winning, though winning the right way is very sweet and can define lives and history. With this, our need for entertainment and competition is met all year round through sport, and thank God for that. And in Ireland that competition is wholesome and compelling, providing talking points, arguments and craic from all quarters. This is a country bred and fed on competitive sport, and I love it.

Ireland has a proud tradition in many international sports, not least boxing and rugby union, and can hold its own in terms of its record in major soccer tournaments. The desire to compete appears inbred, whatever the sport, and there is a real passion and purpose about representing your parish, province or country. Look into the hungry, eager eyes of the Irish middleweight in the Olympics, driven by desire to fight for his family and flag. Watch the Munster Rugby Union team face every game as though it is their last battle of a war that cannot be lost, knowing full well that their community depends on it, especially in hard times. There is a fierce provincial pride, with Thomond Park, Limerick, being the heartbeat, though the bloodline and red-shirted passion reaches out to the whole province. Sport is more than sport in Ireland, if that makes sense. Representing your country, or local community, is something to value dearly – it is very, very close to the heart, whatever the sport. Not least in those unique areas of conflict known as the Gaelic Games.

These are sports played from the grass roots to the highest levels of competition by amateur sportsmen and women. While the GAA has evolved over the years to be an effective and successful business, it aims to plough back money to resource the grass roots game. These are sports where the players do not hold their clubs or counties to ransom through greedy pay demands. Here the concepts of honour, pride and glory prevail. And, furthermore, while that alone makes them alien to professional sports throughout the world, their history and ethos is undoubtedly unique, not rare. However, watching Gaelic football or hurling when you are not reared on it, is a challenge initially. There are some things which take some adjusting to. For example, why does one strong physical challenge receive the referee's whistle when another, perhaps more fearful clash, go unpunished? Also, how do the players manage to dish out constantly intense physical pressure, receive even more of the same, and just get on with the game? There's a culture of just getting on with it, take your stick and dish it out. It's all part of the game, just like it is all part of life. There's a lovely, refreshing feeling that the referee will only stop the game if a head falls off.

The Gaelic Games are embedded in Irish history, a spine of resistance and endurance which holds the character of the country together. They are that important. Take them away and you take a father or mother from a family. By speaking to passionate locals, I have gained some sense of how the games have developed in communities and as part of the nation's identity. These are the games of the Irish people which not only survived the challenges of British occupation, but flourished as a sport and as an everlasting reminder of resistance and the rights to freedom. The murder of innocents at Croke Park, the components of Hill 16 at that same stadium, are but vivid reminders that sport, community and history are entwined in this country. Over the years, each local community would have a story of its own to tell, how Irish life went on despite attempts to stop it. Gaelic Games are more than sport, they are a way of life, and they stretch back in Ireland's history to pull through a golden thread of national pride and achievement. When I saw my first live hurling match between Dublin and Limerick, my eyes locked on to the spectacle, while my mind wandered to the past. There was a sense of a dignified, noble, tribal clash of perfect amateur athletes, pushing skills and legalised aggression to their limits. Hopefully, the meaning of the game, and the ethos, is very much the same as in bygone days. It certainly remains a physically and emotionally brave sport, demanding great team spirit and a will to win.

The fact is that Irish independence has ensured that those playing and watching the games these days can return home without further, more obvious, battles to fight. In darkened, more difficult days, that was not the case. It is a sport of defiance and the truth. For the future, should the true sporting backbone of the GAA remain, I sense all will be well in Ireland. From an outsider looking in, my day in Thurles was again a warm and welcome one. As the crowd sang the National Anthem, I was once again reminded of this country's independence and pride, and was heartened by this. I felt very lucky to be living and working here. As I watched opposing fans of all ages mingle safely and in good humour, it reminded me of the true meaning of sport.

Then, quite naturally, there are those sports which centre on the marriage of man and horse. This is inevitable given the social evolution in Ireland where the horse and other creatures were vital to the way of life. The Irish racing industry is renowned worldwide in terms of breeding and performance on the track. There can be no doubt that the country breeds the best jockeys in Europe, possibly the world. Horsemen filled with an aptitude, and work rate that sets them aside from many others. Instinct and tradition feed a passion to learn and to win, on the flat and over jumps. The horses provide the vehicle to go from flag to post, and are the cornerstone of the whole sport. Go to the Galway Racing Festival in late July and you will clearly see both the glory of sport and the enticement of gambling. Stay in Galway that very week and you will see everyone take part in the festival – those involved in producing rampant sporting action and those enjoying the spectacle as satisfied spectators. It is the highlight of my sporting year, when I sell my soul to the devil once more. Eat, drink and be merry, gamble on Dermot Weld's horses and simply enjoy the craic. Everyone you meet in Galway has an opinion on each race, based on a form book, insider information, or simply the look of the jockey. The whole of Ireland appears to charge to the main stands seconds before the race is 'Off', to witness the competition, then await the result and the familiar sound of 'winner alright, winner alright'. Drink will flow, as will tears of joy and occasional heartbreak. This is life I will surely miss one day. Until then, every year I will book my place in Flannery's Hotel and take the chance that my liver and my wallet will take me through the dream, one more time, just one more time, dear Lord.

While horse racing provides an occasional interest, culminating in the Galway festival, greyhound racing holds a greater part of my heart. My initial journey here was because of Daisy, and through greyhound racing I have met so many wonderful people, all in love with the game and the dogs themselves. Ireland is surely the capital of the greyhound world. The breeding and racing of greyhounds provides great interest and also business in the country. It is a sport which gets into the blood and never leaves while you are able to breathe. I think of breeder – trainers such as the Crotty's, Jane Houfton, Harry Crapper and Larry Bourke himself. Without the dogs, what would their life be? Without such people involved in the game, what quality of life would the dogs have? Even though they would all have reared and raced dogs in their own different ways, they all believe that the welfare of greyhounds is paramount. That is the only fact that really matters in greyhound racing – whether the dog is racing or retired. My good friends, John and Judith Moreton, who work tirelessly for the Retired Greyhound Trust in Sutton on Trent, share the very same fierce principle. Whether you own, train, breed or care for greyhounds, their wellbeing must always come first. After all, these wonderful animals provide dreams and, at times, heartache, but they do this generously and honestly. They depend on us.

Yes, the dreaming starts very early with greyhounds, often before the mating, let alone the whelping! The excitement of a new litter, seeing them play and grow, developing their own unique characters along the way. The challenge of schooling, seeing some take to the game naturally while others struggle.

The unpredictability of the game, like life itself, when breeding might suggest how a dog will develop, but when the reality may be so much different. You can take very little for granted in greyhound racing, perhaps only the fact that these are the most wonderful of animals, each and every one different, but often with some inherited characteristics of their parents. Every greyhound that I have been involved with has given its all on the track and given even more in retirement. They are the funniest, most entertaining and genuine creatures you could meet, and it is an absolute pleasure to give them love and security when they retire.

And Ireland is the home of the breed. It certainly is home again for Daisy. My adventure started with her in Cappawhite with dear old Larry Bourke. I'm not sure whether he is looking down on us in Knockadrehid, but if he is, I'd be certain that he'd take great pleasure in seeing Daisy back home, less than twenty miles away from where he reared her. If only he knew the full story of our adventure and how it has given one very fortunate Welshman a life to savour. It is an adventure in life which owes everything to greyhound racing and Ireland itself. As of today, Daisy and Casey fill my life with so much friendship and love, while my two young pups provide anticipation and hope for the coming years. I've learnt more in recent months about schooling and training dogs than ever before, as these two young pups, Yorkshire Flyer and Trefnant Girl start their racing careers. Watching them learn and develop in the heartland of greyhound racing, in the expert care of Mary and John Crotty, is a joy I will always treasure.

# 10 – John and Mary Crotty

Throughout, John and Mary Crotty have done everything they can to help me settle and enjoy life here. They have been as good and trustworthy friends as you could pray for. Taking the rubbish, delivering coal and bulk dog food, looking after the dogs when I was away and so on. But much more than that as well, not least in their knowledge of greyhounds, especially injuries and sickness. The only time I have had to take a greyhound to the vets so far was to have Ollie put down…and again John took me there and lifted my spirits on the way back as Ollie lay in a blanket, her last breath passed. I recall occasions when the dogs were sick, off their food and within days of 'J. Crotty, Veterinary Services' calling at no cost mind you, they were up and running again. They were so reassuring when it came to the dogs, including when Daisy ripped her inside leg open somewhere in the field. Within weeks she was back to her best. John and Mary always respected my love of the dogs and were happy for the dogs to be in the house when I was in, while we agreed that they needed to be in kennels when I was out. Initially, John built a lovely bench in his large garage, covered from any draft. Then, in the second summer he built a stone kennel and a fenced run so that the dogs could have the most beautiful view of the hills and have the chance to speak to the horses during the day. What a life they have in this sanctuary.

And, of course, John and Mary have helped me learn much about Irish life, now and in the past. They'd spent well over twenty years in England as a young married couple, having gone there to find work in the previous depression. In those days it was natural, almost expected that people would cross the Irish Sea to find work. Many stayed and some came home. While John values the financial benefits of his stay in England, he also regrets missing those years away from family and his beautiful village, O'Brien's Bridge. Yet he developed all his building skills in England. He went there as a labourer and through close observation learning, watching bricklayers and other skilled workers, he became self-taught. The beautiful curved wall entrance at the house is testament to his skill and should remain a landmark memorial to John, down the Killaloe Road. He certainly is a grafter. His retirement day will be the same day as they screw the lid down on his coffin. He is a very practical man and a wise one at that. Someone who clearly has not let life pass him by as a learning experience. Yes, and, of course, he can tell a tale well and is very, very good company. More than this, he is a compassionate man who values animal life and those less fortunate than himself.

On my occasional days off, John will pop up for coffee and we'll talk about life now and life past. It has sparked a real interest in Irish history as I frequently try to imagine life in the area at different times. As a proud Welshman, encouraged by my mother and Uncle Ken, I always had an interest in history. But the history I was taught in school was from a British perspective. The Empire, our teachers consistently told us, was a fact, something which happened because it had to. To enlighten others, to lead and to develop trade, industry and employment for all. That was the message that every school taught in my youth. Yet, being Welsh, with an interest in where I came from, I always looked further. One nation does not enter another by chance, nor out of charity. Consequently, as time passed in my new homeland, I not only appreciated the natural beauty and way of life, but I questioned how Irish people must have felt over the years, under British rule.

Both in and out of work, my experiences made me wonder how life must have been at different stages in Irish history, in the Bridge, in Limerick city, in the prison and in the parishes. Above all, I wondered what it must have been like to be free in my own, very beautiful, country, before invaders took away land and that freedom. What it was like to have laws imposed by aliens whose culture and values were so far away from mine. What life was like paying taxes for little or no return, being left to die in a famine and for being told how to speak and which games to play. What life was like, and how life escalated through wars and depressions, through emigration to far off worlds. And I wonder, after all this loss and much more, why do Irish people remain so warm and spirited towards visitors even though their own scars of freedom fighting are so fresh? I came to the conclusion that, because of their history, rather than despite it, the Irish are a rare breed. There's nothing like them, nothing like their way of life – and this despite eight hundred years of oppression and fight. To win their own world war against one of the world's most powerful empires, is a glorious liberation and everlasting achievement in itself. To keep your character, dignity, humility and sense of humour through that mammoth struggle appears seemingly impossible, but, they've achieved it.

Yes, they have kept their own way, and thank God for that. As for the Church, for all the modern day essential revelations of clerical abuse, it must not be forgotten that each man and woman is responsible for his actions – both the abuser and those who have colluded and denied the truth. It is easy to hide behind an organisation, whether it be a Roman one or a London-based one. And while the Catholic Church begins its rehabilitation in this respect, it can still hold its head high for its role in keeping communities spiritually uplifted and resourced by God, for the many years in the battle for freedom.

Yes, and while I would discuss history and tradition with John, Mary would take a more pragmatic, modern view, believing that time should move on, without lingering on the past. Maybe their views reflect those of many Irish families today, coping with modern day practicalities, yet holding dear to them the memories of the past. I think that is vital in Ireland today and it will be more so in the future. Tradition and culture are the backbone of this nation. In England, however, the past and traditions seem to be swept aside by a thing called progress. My English friends sometimes don't know what being English is anymore; it got lost in the pay-packet, amidst a thing called liberalism and through an excuse to put away honesty, called political correctness. The pride my English friends have in their country is often questioned by those who care nothing for traditional communities. Progress, it seems, almost prostitutes a community's heritage, and that of a nation, regardless of what the past has been. Whether your country's deeds have been shameful or distinguished, surely you must be free to debate the issues, to seek the truth of your past, present and future. Some may say that this is no longer the British way but, thank God, it can still be a way for the Irish. But one thing is for sure, the Crotty's optimism for life and their sense of humour is what I perceive as being typically Irish. I could just imagine the world crumbling into dust and the economy hitting even harder than it has. Yet John and Mary would still be as optimistic and believing as ever.

Their life is constant in terms of how they care about each other and others. John's ability to build is as reliable as his readiness to listen and consider. He would make a very good probation officer, though I wouldn't tell him that as he thinks it is an easy job with too many holidays! He could inspire someone by setting an example. Just as he learnt his fine skills watching and listening in the building trade in England, those around him could learn a thing or two simply by watching and taking note. He could inspire someone to write a book. As for Mary, her heart is as good and honest as John's, and as generous. If she sees a stray dog, she does not walk by. If she sees someone in need or trouble, again she does not ignore the truth. She has the devil about her and can match John punch for punch when it comes to devilment. They're as much angels as good people, though they would walk me to the bog and bury me six feet under, with the rest of the English soldiers, if I suggested that. Somehow God put two very good people together and it simply got better. One thing is for sure...they don't know how important they have been in my life. I know I have gained so much from living here and I hope I have returned the goodwill, in some ways at least, by looking after and cherishing their home on the Killaloe Road.

# 11 – Doing Time

I know there was great reluctance by many Probation Officers to serve their time in a prison environment. But I was quite happy to go into Limerick Prison to work, having previously completed a two year stint in HMP Wakefield. Prison gives you the chance to share perspectives and values as you work with a range of professionals. Plus, of course, it was an eye opener for me seeing things done the Irish way within their legal system. While the concrete, stone and metal are similar constructs and constraints to HMP Wakefield, working in Limerick Prison is far closer to actually working in the local community. The prison accommodates those remanded in custody by the courts, plus short to long term prisoners including Lifers. The robust and impregnable walls, which I saw in the company of Larry Bourke on my first night in Ireland, are exactly that. Solid and steadfast. But they are also only a skin between life in this fascinating city and life in prison.

Thankfully, life in Her Majesty's Prison Wakefield had taught me a few things which I held on to. First, security and safety were paramount. Secondly, prison is the Governor's house and if you are told to jump, you do it and accept it. Thirdly, despite prison life surviving on a diet of professionalism and discipline, if you don't have a sense of humour you will not survive. Taking those well-proven principles from Europe's biggest high security prison into one of Ireland's most demanding and challenging was my life saver. I soon found out that ways were different here, which, once more, proved to be a breath of fresh air in my life.

I tried to learn fast in terms of processes and procedures as I simply had to. I also learnt that despite the professionalism of staff, you could have some fun too. Limerick Prison puts a unique strain on staff and I have always admired how they conduct themselves professionally in terms of getting the job done, treating prisoners with respect and keeping discipline. Staff have this unique knack of providing a constructive, humanitarian environment within a controlled unit based on safety and security. A blend of rules and regulations alongside the principle of human dignity. This works here. This works well in a prison where most inmates know most officers, directly or indirectly, through family or community links. The 'form lines' held by experienced prison staff are impressive. Officers may know a prisoner and they may also know his father, who was a good musician, the mother whose brother committed suicide and the greyhound they produced to run in the Limerick St Leger. Of course, this can sometimes be problematic when trying to assess risk and motivation as personal knowledge and community influences can occasionally affect judgement. But I can see the benefits too, especially when these officers are as professional and disciplined as you would want. Saying that, professional staff of all disciplines, they may be…but this doesn't mean that character and humour are lost along the way.

One tall, dark and handsome officer, discretely known as O'Dea, is but one example where hard-nosed professionalism meets warmth and humour. He has his formalised duties as an officer and his informal duties as a morale booster. I'm sure both are in his job description and he's been very well-trained to meet both calls. Officer O'Dea spends any occasional spare time touring the prison making sure no one is slacking on duty. He will be heard drifting down corridors talking to himself or the walls.

"I'm under fierce pressure and nobody cares, he would often say." He's had to learn refined techniques over the past thirty years to reduce the pressures of the job. These techniques include talking sport, taking the mickey and lifting morale. He earns every penny for this. He frequently praises the 'school of excellence', the medical unit. Every time he visits, he gives heart-warming commendations to those excellent staff with a medical remit, who handle wayward prisoners with either kid gloves or a rod of verbal steel. He treats the Nursing Manager with great respect. "Yes, Matron, I'll see to that for you, of course." Then, when she has gone, it is often a case of 'the good Matron wants more staff, she's a slim chance in hell."

Yes, Officer O'Dea makes his way from office to office, always welcomed by staff because of the craic he brings. Whenever he enters my room and the Prison Chaplain is present, it is the usual comment, "Ar'Jees, the two biggest rogues in the prison, fiddling the priests takings or the sweepstake again." He spread the tale of the 'real reason' that I left the UK…wanted by Interpol for match fixing, on the run from vengeful husbands, whose wives had been swindled into bed and swindled out of pearls and diamonds. He'd talk of 'Wanted' posters being put up in Holyhead and Fishguard and he spread the rumour of me having plastic surgery to look like a benign man of God instead of a 'spiv from North Wales'. He accused me of favouring blonde ladies in the sweepstakes, brunettes in the Christmas Raffle and anyone who would buy me a pork pie or a pint of Guinness. Any hopes of me having an honourable reputation in Limerick Prison were dashed by my good friend, O'Dea.

When we had the sweepstake for the 2010 World Cup, our leader, Officer O'Dea, and the Chaplain placed themselves on the organising committee with myself. I was keen to organise the event and asked for two reputable characters to help out. Someone, understandably put the priest's name forward while others set me up by suggesting O'Dea. I now realise how vulnerable and innocent I was entering the prison walls. While I expected some of the prisoners to try and take advantage of me, I never thought I'd have too much trouble with occasionally roguish staff. When I first met Officer O'Dea, I remember thinking what a nice, friendly man, a gentleman. Someone you could definitely trust. Now, looking back, I'd trust that likeable rogue as much as I'd trust a rattlesnake in my wellies!

I should have been forewarned that running a sweepstake with O'Dea, regardless of the Chaplain's presence on the committee, was doomed to failure. Once the money was collected, the draw was made, amid accusation of fixed and fiddled. Nevertheless the competition started, stretching for over four weeks. Within days, the results on the wall chart were being wrongly entered. It was O'Dea, of course, but I couldn't prove it. Then he started the rumour that I was fixing the score chart in favour of female colleagues, particularly 'the one wee blondie who you have eyes for'. Then, within days, he came to see me 'on a matter of integrity and utmost privacy'.

He said that we needed to act quickly so as to protect the credibility of the sweepstake, especially given the vast prize fund. He then proceeded to disclose that the Chaplain and an officer had 'fiddled' the draw by breaking the competition rules…the priest apparently having sold one of his two teams to the officer after the competition had started and without the committee's agreement. When I said it wasn't the worst offence, O'Dea pulled me up sharp, saying that if we let the priest get away with this one and it became public, our own personal reputations would be finished! He then added that there was only one answer. The breach of rules was so blatant that the priest must be fined one hundred euros, which had to be shared directly between the charities of the two remaining committee members (myself and O'Dea), and that the good father must be removed from the committee. I had to agree, of course, but I pointed out a fundamental flaw – we had no written rules, so how could the priest be in breach and ex-communicated?

"Ah, sure, never sweat the small things…I'm sure you'll find the rules by tomorrow morning." And so I did, using my imagination!

Though that wasn't the last of it. The next day, the priest was publicly carpeted for breaching rule 6a, having read and signed the rules previously. However, he couldn't remember reading or signing the rules at all and insisted on seeing the evidence. Confidently, in front of half-a-dozen witnesses, I produced the rule book with his signature giving apparent fact to the accusation that he knowingly breached the rules…got ya! For a moment, O'Dea looked over with that sinister, warm but weasily glint in his eye, asking for the one hundred euros from the Prison Priest.

"Pay up, Father, you've been found out, don't make it worse for yourself." But as the priest shook his head and peered at the signature, he noticed the date on the document.

"Hold on, hold on, this says I signed it when I was away in Poland! How did the Good Lord manage that one then!" At this point O'Dea gave me the accusing glance that Fagan would have given Oliver Twist. Our Chaplain was smarter than we thought or maybe the Good Lord intervened at the right time. Either way, the charge was dropped on a technicality and O'Dea's latest scam went astray.

After this, O'Dea then tried to make further capital, this time from myself. When the competition ended, we had set aside a time for the prize presentation. I had the prize money but was pulled away to attend an urgent meeting. In front of half-a-dozen witnesses, I approached O'Dea and passed on the prize money, slowly counting it all out in front of the security cameras. Later that day, as Nurse Siobhan waited for her winnings, our good friend, Officer O'Dea, said he could not pay her because the Welshman, myself, still had the prize money. He denied that I had given him the money earlier, claiming that I still had the cash. When asked to check the transaction on camera, mysteriously or rather through some managerial influence, the camera tape was not in play that day. O'Dea then kept Siobhan waiting for two weeks before she was paid, then claimed that he paid her out of his own pocket. He became a hero while I was discredited as he told everyone that I used the money for a seedy holiday in Bangkok, a place I have never been in my life!

Yes, in a close knit community, such as prison, humour is important and it seems that everyone contributes. Dr Tim, the resident Psychologist, is as professional and compassionate a man that you could meet, and he joined in the banter too. With the Prison Chaplain, he offered his services as my fashion and image consultant. Those two gave advice on hairstyle and grooming in general, encouraging me to stop pulling my pants up as though my braces had bust. Between them they tried to marry me off, acting as a dating agency, unsuccessfully I might add! I think Dr Tim and the priest still see my future marriage to an Irish lass as the peak of their professional ambition, certainly as image consultants. However, as Officer Finbar once said, "You can't put in what God left out."

Then there is the prison dentist, warmly termed over the years as 'The Butcher'. He is a class act, able to do his difficult job whilst making it look easy. A highly skilled professional, who, in no shape or form, should be termed a butcher. While the priest is the most respected man in the prison and O'Dea the 'biggest rogue', 'the Butcher' is the most feared. If you, a prisoner, decide to put your name forward for his free service, you also put your life in his rubber-gloved hands! My first contact with the dentist was when I heard him release another victim with a typically joyful despatch.

"Off you go then, be careful who you kiss tonight as they might fall out." I then saw the victim walk, head down into the holding cell, tissue to his mouth and already regretting having had the treatment. As he sat down on the bench, face to face with two mature prisoners, he bravely fought back the tears. One wise old lag peered over and menacingly whispered, "All I want for Christmas is mi two front teeth," at which point Officer Carey simply blasted, "Next, please,

Gentlemen!" Macho minded prisoners often enter the dentist's chair as hard men but are then reminded of their true limitations.

Yes, if a prison officer tells you to do something, you do it. If a Governor asks you to do any job, you do it. Providing its ethical, of course. Yet, despite their highly responsible role, Limerick Prison Governors are human too. They seem to be respected by both staff and the prisoners. Maybe it's their down to earth approach, a 'no snobbery here' outlook and the fact that their lengthy experience has bred respect. Mind you, despite the heavy stresses of their job, managing safety and security, there are lighter moments. Review meetings are classic examples of this, adding a flavour of the warmth, community and humour that Ireland is famous for.

"Good morning, folks, you're as welcome as the first flowers in May," calls Governor Mullane in a typically warm and welcoming style. He could make a condemned man feel valued at the gallows such is his charm. The meeting gets underway, reviewing the good, the bad and the ugly. Assessing the risk, telling the tale of O'Neill's father and mother, who, if you believed the rumours, not only served sentences here but somehow managed to combine to create young O'Neill on the premises! Then Governor O'Riordan himself, head down opening his papers while others talked...

"Well, I've seen it all now,'' he said as he opened a warrant on a new committal... The judge has remanded Willie Maughan for the month and has set him two pieces of homework! First, he needs to write a piece on the history of the Black and Tans in Ireland...then he has to explain the origins of the word 'Wanker'!

As we all laughed instantly, we felt the warmth and humour in the room and no doubt valued, once again, the break from our duties. And as for another valued member of staff, he was happy enough to use history to make me feel part of the team and I was happy enough to take the comment as a warm welcome of acceptance. I remember pushing a point on a particular case, a high risk offender, who should not be released early, for obvious reasons.

"Jees," he said. "Here we go again. We put up with British rule for eight hundred years and here you are again telling us what to do." He'd repeat the eight hundred year comment many times in the following years, appropriately and humorously and I always respected him for trusting my sense of humour on each occasion. That touch of honesty, never hiding the true facts of history but using them warmly, made me feel very welcome.

And, of course, there would be a million tales told by officers during their careers inside and, of course, they would always be totally true. Including the tale of Sean O'Leary as told by Orderly Hogan in the medical team. A regular customer of the prison, O'Leary was subject to suicide watch as he struggled to cope with his current incarceration. Officer Hogan, a man known for both compassion and endearing sarcasm, was sent to try and cheer O'Leary up.

"Try to be positive, Sean…see that man there, the poor sod with the limp and miserable face. He's in here for having intercourse with a donkey and getting caught in the act by the missis." O'Leary stood, timeless and speechless as Officer Hogan moved on to his next compassionate duty. Time passed and for many years Sean O'Leary was never seen in Cork or Limerick Prison. It was as though he was dead. Then over 10 years down the line, Officer Hogan and his good lady were shopping in Ennis. Being 6'2", eyes of blue and having a presence to un-nerve any audience, Hogan pushed his trolley between the bakery and the fresh strawberries only to bump into a chiselled old face, accompanied by a woman and two children. As O'Leary spotted the unmistakeable Officer Hogan, he rushed to him, shaking his head and grabbing his hand. In instant tears of gratification, he said, "I'm so pleased to see you, so grateful for you saving my life." Hogan, totally aghast, asked what was he talking about? Of course…it was the tale of the prisoner who had sex with the donkey… "I'm off the drink for years, back with the wife, working and keeping out of trouble. You made me realise that I was a lucky fecker when you told me about the man who had to have sex with the old donkey. I've got the wife and I never appreciated her until you told me that." It's a funny old world.

And there are many other characters within these walls, durable and wise through over thirty years of service, including Chief O'Sullivan. On the face of it the Chief could be described as a rough diamond. His occasionally abrasive stance can ruffle a feather or two and he can appear to be a hard man, governed by the rules and regulations. He will stand his corner and only a fool would rush into a fight with him. But beneath the front is a warm, very fair and understanding man and I soon grew to enjoy his company and welcomed his support on many occasions.

Yes, he has a traditional view on life, expressed with rural wit and always a tinge of devilment rather than any intent to offend. A wise man, far deeper than he would want you to see. One day a diabetic prisoner was refusing to take his insulin. The Chief was called. "I'll not take it, never again, don't waste your time persuading me," the inmate told him. Giving nothing away with his blank expression, the Chief said:

"No, you are right. I'd be wasting my time, I see you have your mind set. Fair enough. I'll do my best for you, sort the arrangements and the rest." He broke for a brief few seconds and then asked the prisoner:

"But do me a favour, write a will in case I'm not back for a while. I'll pick it up later." The Chief then went about his business elsewhere, the medical officers doing likewise. Within minutes the prisoner roared for attention, telling the Class Officer, "OK, I'll take my injection." Calling his bluff was smarter than the prisoner trying to manipulate the situation and proved that a wise act can come in many guises. Like most hard men, Chief O'Sullivan's soft and generous nature is well hidden but only a fool cannot see his honesty and compassion.

Yes, Limerick Prison can be a testing and demanding community, left to others to manage while the world nearby outside goes on regardless. I will always remember the sound of the alarm when officer's gallop to the action and civilian staff press flat to the walls to avoid the hoof prints. The aim for those who work inside prison is to go in and come out safely, day after day. For those detained there, for some it is hell, others home and for many an occupational hazard. For myself, it has been a privilege to work there amongst so many decent and professional people and to have the opportunity to try and contribute to a community that the rest of the world sometimes forgets. I doubt whether the quality of compassionate professionalism could be surpassed in any other institution.

# 12 – The City with a Beating Heart

This is the city affectionately known as stab city. In 2008 Limerick was classed as the murder capital of Western Europe. It's long-term history includes numerous foreign invasions, tribal warfare, King John and eight hundred years of painful British rule, the Black and Tans, plus the successful fight to ensure Irish freedom. It also means 'the Limerick feuds' and their growth into gangland vendettas. This is a beautiful city to the eye, in most parts, offering some classic architecture, symbolic churches, a wet mouth to a beautiful ocean and a once prosperous dockland. It is also a city of renowned spirit and humour, a close knit 'village' where people still know their neighbours and their enemies. Along with Cork, it provides the home of Munster Rugby, the modern flag bearer of the area's fighting spirit, roaring to the beating chant of 'Stand up and Fight'. A rugby province that reflects the character of the ordinary or rather special people of the area…looking the enemy in the eye, unflinching and determined, playing each game to the eighty-first minute, never giving up. Life is sharp and sweet in Limerick with a vibrant edge. I can imagine a world without many places but not without Limerick City.

A man from another major city once described Limerick as a dysfunctional family that will never fade into history, despite its problems. I love the life of the place despite the deaths of the place. It's a battleground where life sometimes goes back to the basics to the sharpest end. How it coped with British rule without losing its heart and character, I'll never know. Perhaps, the brutal history of occupation is the reason why Limerick people and the Irish generally are so proud and resilient. What life was like here in the courts and the prison, those many years ago, I can only guess. There must have been constant fear, rage and hatred against an illegally occupying force. Of course life evolved under British rule and life went on. But how this community and others in Ireland, survived the threat to their self-belief and unique character, I will never know. I walk the streets, very proud to work here and contribute in some small way. To date I have never received any abuse because of my own heritage. Yet I know about the insults, abuse and discrimination suffered by Irish people in the UK. Something is wrong there and something is wonderfully right here.

There will, however, be a place and a time that will struggle to welcome a Welshman or a Brit, which is wholly understandable. I am aware of the passionate republicanism that runs through many veins and I am with that totally. If this was my land and my family's home was burnt to the ground because they couldn't pay the rent, how would I react? If the Black and Tans dragged my forefathers into the street to brutalise and kill them simply because of their rightful belief in freedom in their own land, how would I respond? If my own people had died through a famine and been abandoned by the British Government, how should I feel about such a government, such an occupying force? If my own culture and way of life was taken away by people from a different culture and way of life, I would obviously feel pain and anger at the very least. I can understand why the allegiance they had to give to another country's Queen was not given or given reluctantly and why they wear the Irish tricolour on their biceps. And in Limerick many do and many have sat across my desk in Limerick Prison, seeking help or making plans to turn their life around. They must see me and those like me as the outsider, a remnant of a different age. Most would come from the most deprived areas of the city, the pockets of poverty. All would have grown up hardened by their experience but yet warm and humorous, even soft in centres. Their forefathers' experience in this rich and tasty city will be marked by a history of oppression. Yet it will be soaked in resilience and a unique national character which Irish people have taken all over the world. Maybe it is that character, built on Ireland's painful and glorious past, that keeps the city's heart beating, whatever the difficulties.

I vividly recall a discussion with a thirty-year-old male prisoner. His life had been spent in care since the age of eight. Alcoholic parents, his father dying when the child was seven, the mother living the rest of her days looking through the bottom of a glass. An only child needing love and guidance but only receiving abuse from those who should have cared. Placed in homes where dark rooms meant dark secrets. Where the indecent touch from a member of staff was considered the norm and part and parcel of life. Such was life at that time, fostering mistrust and anger, leading to juvenile crime, drug addiction and escalating violence. From head-butts to slashings to a love affair with guns and gangs, the only things he could rely on. This became his family.

But even they let you down in the end and as he comes to terms with another prison sentence, he wonders why. And despite his disadvantages of family and fate and despite the mess he has made of life so far, he makes his plans. Somewhere there is a spark and he begins to look forward. He becomes drug free and thinks there may be a future. Within the prison walls he creates his own space, putting up barriers against those who damn him and doubt him. He educates himself and educates others through his progress. I asked him where he got this drive and direction from. He said, "It's inside but also outside." Despite every disadvantage heaped on him and every disastrous decision he made to make his life worse, he found that his environment could help him in the end.

"Limerick is different, Terry. It nearly killed me but it has made me as well." The city may have been his downfall but it may also be his salvation.

While for me, I am one of the lucky ones. I may serve a sentence in the day time but I am free at night. By the time I am nearing home, the stresses have eased away and life today, and hopefully tomorrow, revolves around Knockadrehid and O'Brien's Bridge.

# 13 – Today and Tomorrow

Today was a holiday. Amanda, John and the family had just set off back after the Easter festivities. Seeing them, Nic, Paul, Gwynne, Cheryl and the four girls was a lovely break. We didn't go far, no farther than Killaloe and Castleconnell. No need to. They now realise that my heart is here and they can see why. When they left I walked to the village in the baking heat. I popped into Bonners and bumped into Tessie, a seventy year old lady, and a man with apple rosy cheeks and an angel's smile. We talked about old Christy with pleasure and with many fond tales. The fondness for him was comforting, reflecting the warmth of a close community that cared for its own. Then Tessie offered me some strawberry sponge cake to go with my lunchtime Guinness which I gladly accepted. It would be rude to say 'no', Tessie.

"It would, for sure," she replied. "After all, it has Viagra in the baking, that's what makes it rise." We giggled and enjoyed our time and cake, thinking of Christy and thinking of life. Then Christy Murphy joined us, warmly blackguarding old Christy, describing him as the biggest liar in the village. Though he could say the same about anyone who crossed the pub threshold including himself.

"Do you fish, Terry?" he asked.

"No, not since I was a nipper."

"Well, you must try now you're here on holiday."

Margaret interrupted by saying, "Hold on now, Christy, Terry lives here on the Killaloe Road in John Crotty's house." I confirmed this and I said I was 'blown in' over two years ago, hence the term 'a blow in'.

"Oh, no, you're not, you're one of us now," said the man with apple rosy cheeks and an angel's smile. While it isn't quite the case and may never be, I felt the warmth and acceptance in his comments and went home a very happy man.

Yes, today I am a very happy man as I have been every day since I moved to Ireland. Of course there have been difficult days and many times that I have sensed the anguish of my Irish friends as they cope with the recession. The suffering of ordinary people is very real. I have seen the impact in financial terms in the last few years. Less in the pocket, endless and seemingly unfair taxation and redundancies. If we believed the media and politicians, we would think Ireland is just an economy, not a great country. Thankfully, there is something about Irish people that does not allow them to get down and stay down. Maybe it is easier for me to see as I look in from the outside. I look around at a beautiful country, everywhere you go, and I live amongst people whose richness is so apparent to me but not always to themselves. Sometimes I wonder if I see a different Ireland than my Irish friends, often having to remind them that they are God's chosen few and could not be in a better place. I suppose it comes down to your perspective of life and that in itself depends on your own life history and that of your environment. Consequently, while I can see a very obvious naked beauty in this wonderful country, I also try to imagine how the Irish see their world, their past and present in particular. While every Irishman or woman has their own perspective, there must be some common strands which bind their culture together, ensuring that whatever the situation, they will survive.

Yes, my today is as good as I could wish for. I hope tomorrow will be the same. My own past makes me the man I am and constructs those images I have of people and the world. Moving to Ireland has allowed me to make sense of things, many things including myself. I know my own limits, what I have pride in and what I am ashamed of. I am content with this, so content that this will be my home for as long as God wants me to be here. Yet, I am a proud Welshman who benefitted from a Yorkshire education in life in all respects. I was lucky to live in Yorkshire and enjoy many of life's experiences for so long. In my opinion, Yorkshire people have a blunt homely character and a Yorkshire grit which forms the spine of the country. However, despite my forty-five years of Yorkshire life, I have never seen myself as an Englishman, rather a proud Welshman abroad. The same applies, today and tomorrow as I live in Ireland…a proud Welshman abroad. Yes, I am proud of that. What I am not proud of is British history in Ireland.

My time since moving here enlightens me in this respect. It's got me asking questions about the past as I now doubt the history they taught me in school. I've found myself learning about Ireland's past and present, in particular the role of Britain in this. While you cannot change events of the past, you can reconsider and re-write history to reflect the truth. And, of course, we can stop teaching that invasion and occupation was either glorious or justified. It was neither of these.

So, for now, I sit in my Irish Heaven, the birds entertaining me while Daisy and Casey ramble to their hearts content. As is often the case I count my good fortune, my blessings, knowing that I have been given the chance to see things differently before it is too late and to have my share of paradise on earth. I think of tomorrow and hope life goes on much the same, unfussed, simple and at a pace I can now endure. Yet I think of the past more and more. Not because I see no future but I think the past helps me understand many truths, my own personal truths and others. When you live in a rat race like I did, the mirror is just something to shave in. Now, it is a chance to reflect in every sense, to consider what is important. As for the future of Ireland, this will depend on how Ireland sees itself and how the world sees Ireland. Looking into the mirror, Ireland may not yet see the truth. That fact is that Ireland is a beautiful country and a great one at that. Great, because it has endured and overcome countless challenges, bringing with it a character which is loved and respected worldwide.

Hopefully, as times evolve, those who have broken the hearts of this wonderful country will understand the truth of the past. Not to keep wounds open but to help them heal. In the coming years, Ireland will commemorate its greatest victories to date and the everlasting cornerstone of their nation. Those who suffered and died for a peaceful tomorrow, deserve to have a growing and lasting peace.

# 14 – All Because of Daisy

So, was it really 'All because of Daisy' that I came to Ireland to stay? Well, if it was not for Daisy and my love of greyhound racing, I would never have experienced that initial Irish hospitality at the hands of Larry and Babs Bourke. That brief trip was an opportunity we all need in life but sometimes never take. Luck is a priceless commodity and I have been very lucky. I sensed Ireland was love at first sight and so it has proved to be. Though this has been no brief encounter, no holiday romance. In this story, this personal account, I have unravelled for myself the reasons for my journey to Ireland and the reasons why I stay. Looking at my personal past has not been easy. Honesty rarely is and perspectives of past experiences change. I can now see that life around the time of Mum's death had become consistently grey, without colour and nourishment. Some days were black. One bereavement, one loss after another in too short a time had drained me and I didn't need a doctor or a friend at the time to tell me I was struggling. I kept it to myself like a dark secret. Sometimes in life we are alive but not living and this was my life at the time. No innocence, no dreams and no hope. I can see it much clearer now. Then, in Ireland, a dream became a reality. Thankfully, I was lucky enough to have a supportive family, more luck than I deserve and more than my share of very good Irish friends, particularly John and Mary Crotty. Without knowing it, they have become my Irish family.

When I moved to Ireland I arrived with no promises to myself other than to have an open mind and to be prepared to change my view of life. I live every day and laugh every day. I see things differently in terms of my own life and history itself, questioning and wondering, imagining and dreaming. I remember being told in school that studying history can help you understand the past, explain the present and help prepare for the future. Only since being here can I honestly consider my own past, understand my life as it is and look to the future. Only by coming to this great country have I been able to seriously question my own country's past actions and the true impact this had on others for so long. This has been the start of a voyage of discovery. If I had never come to this beautiful country, how limited and grey my life would have been to the end. Yet, for whatever reason, I am here and my life is painted in colour again. I can see many things for the first time and I can see other things so very differently than before.

Tonight, I sit on the stone in the far corner of Crotty's field, feet away from the murmuring river and miles away from my working day. Autumn colours provide glowing make up for the trees and the dampened, thick grass freshens the air as it always does. In the centre of the field the horses charge as they play, as free as they would ever want to be. Daisy and Casey rest nearby in the middle of their evening stroll and their happiness is as obvious as mine. I am as free as I could ever wish to be. I have found an appreciation of life and contentment itself. My existence is simple and yet it is my most prized possession. I have no expectations and no more pointless ambitions. I never really knew what I wanted or needed in life until I came here. My dream has become my reality and I have found my own personal truths, peace and contentment.

It all reminds me of the miner, trapped underground with plenty of time to contemplate. He began to think of the important things in his life, his family, his freedom, the love and simplicity of it all. The things that really mattered to him that he had often taken for granted. He dreamed of seeing a light from the rescue party. In time and after all his waiting and mental suffering that light appeared and he was rescued. He then began to try and live his life in fresh awareness of what really was important to him. He swore never to turn off that light, that light of awakening and rescue, now that he had found it…now I feel exactly the same. Yes, I owe much to that very first journey to Ireland to see my beloved Daisy. However, it is because of Ireland itself, the people and their way of life, that I stay.

## THE END…
Or maybe the end of the beginning…